HAPPINESS TO THE RESCUE!

Life Lessons to Survive Everything and be Deliriously Happy

Clara Young, Ph.D.

Neurotic Midlife Crisis, Depression, Cancer and Life Survivor

Happiness to the Rescue!

Contents

For Courageous People

Seeking
a soulful journey
a timeless beauty
to tell the untold story
to release the Gods& Goddesses inside you
to forgive
to honor the loss
to heal the wounded soul
to help, give, and save those who cannot
to find sisterhood & brotherhood
to shape a unique and brilliant life
and to
Have fun, celebrate & share the one & only you in the universe.
Bring respect for self & others, & an open mind, & an unbiased
heart.
Thank you.

Dr. Clara

Introduction

I awoke to a cool summer day.

It was sunny outside and the sky was blue as can be. I drove to my favorite cliff overlooking the beckoning dark blue ocean. Everyone was outside basking in the sun and I could hear the giggles of children running around and playing, deliriously happy, while dogs barked and chased them. The grown-ups were slowly sinking into their plastic chairs for a long- awaited break with a cool drink, while lovers nearby held hands and smooched without shame. Everybody was happy. Everyone, but one. I stood at the edge of the cliff with tears streaming down my face. Nobody noticed.

You couldn't find anyone more unhappy and downright miserable than yours truly. That had been my norm as long as I could remember. Not only did I suffer from clinical depression with all its symptoms blaring and tormenting me for more than 20 years, in a constant state of emptiness, hopelessness, and thoughts of suicide every day, but I was also diagnosed with the most aggressive and rare form of breast cancer with limited treatment options. And during treatment, I ended up referring my patients out, losing my psychotherapy practice and my livelihood, and ended up living in a garage. My life savings drained to cover outrageous medical bills and daily living expenses. At the same time, aging and menopause made a grand entrance with hot flashes, mood swings, and disco hormones, more than happy to humiliate me in public on a daily basis.

Not surprisingly, my depression, which took years to manage, returned with an irresistible vengeance. I had been hit so fast, so hard, one after another; I went into complete shock and became physically and emotionally numb, and I ended up having a breakdown and shut down. I froze for awhile, a long while. What does one do with all this? I had no great insight into this madness. I didn't know what to do. Life was hard enough as it was and then all this.

I sat looking out my window as my body slowly healed from the cancer treatment, which had its own nightmarish side effects. As I felt so defeated and beaten up, only one thought came into my mind over and over. "Get busy living or get busy dying!" The answer evaded me. So, I flipped a coin.

More than anything, cancer changed my life's perspective. I saw everything differently whether I wanted to or not. I couldn't go back to my old life, nor did I want to, because it was such a negative, toxic, and an unhappy one. Besides, time, mortality, and death were front and center now. I had to find my true life and live it before it was all gone. *But how? Kind of a tall order here. Hello?!*

Happiness was the furthest thing from my mind, as it has been for a long time (like, since I was 9!). Like most people, I was working like crazy and waiting for happiness, believing that if I worked hard, followed the rules, and behaved, some things, and the right people, at the right time would make me happy. How foolish was that?! That all got thrown out the window, along with waiting. I don't do waiting any more. Because I've discovered I don't have all the time in the world.

After awhile, my dogs handed me a flyer and insisted that I attend a breast cancer support group, as they grew tired of listening to my problems, sobbing and blubbering, while holding them hostage. They needed a break. Attending a BC support group and listening to others, as well as myself, out loud made me realize a lot of important things crucial to my survival and sanity, and it led me on a self-discovery journey to find my life and what the heck I was supposed to do with it. And then, it hit me.

I got angry. Then, I got really, really pissed off!
I avoided asking the "why me" question as long as I could. But a year after my cancer diagnosis, I had to get it out of my system in order to move on, because it was always hanging around me like an unwelcomed relative. "Why me?!!!" I said it out loud. Nothing made sense, you see, because I was a vegetarian, exercised, didn't eat junk food, didn't drink soda, didn't smoke, wasn't obese, hardly drank alcohol, and had no family history of breast cancer. So what up?!!
I let out a long sigh. I felt like a fool. Why was I expecting anything in life to make sense? I guess I was still green in some ways.

While I was fuming with steam coming out of my ears, I had an epiphany. "The hell with everything!" I screamed and threw my arms in the air. I decided to let go and toss out all the "shoulds" and "supposed tos" and do whatever I wanted for the first time in my life. Being responsible, compromising, sacrificing and doing the right thing my whole life didn't work, so what have I got to lose? Then there was absolute silence. I was baffled. "What is that?" I did not know what I wanted to do. Can you believe it?! For more than 50 years, I've been doing what I was supposed to do; what I was told to do by my cultures, society, peers, and people, dead and alive.

So, what do "I" want to do? How could I not know? I was overwhelmed with sadness, that I had lost touch with myself in life so deeply. I wept, ate some cake, and talked to my dogs, again. I asked myself, "Why did I treat myself so badly with my one and only life? Did I think I had all the time in the world? I wasted most of it on what?" I stood up and said, "No more. Starting now!" My dogs started wagging their tails. Hooray!

I spent the next several years working on finding my real and true life; the one **I WANTED TO LIVE**. It took a while because a lot got in the way. I had to rummage through decades, perhaps a lifetime of emotional garbage, anxiety, self-hatred, societal brainwashing, depression, fear of recurrence, and endless voices of criticism, saying that I'm no good and I won't make it, and I don't deserve it, and *on and on.* After all, I had to go against what the "norm" was for someone like me at my age. Many times, my demons had me by the throat, as I succumbed to its dark voices: "You can't do it, you loser!" Plus, I was always physically exhausted from my cancer treatment, which made it tougher. I trembled for awhile, wept some more, and then I said, "Oh Yeah! Watch me!"

At first, I was like, "*Whoa*, where did that come from?" Then a very loud inner voice said, "I am battling cancer, depression, poverty, aging, and insanity, so what the hell do I care?" Soon, my survival instinct kicked in and I got angry again and then I got up and kept moving. I finally made a promise to myself. I chose to get busy living.

No one told me that the easy part of the cancer journey was the surgery, treatments, being nuked, dealing with endless doctors, appointments, and being infuriated by my health insurance companies. Nope. That was the "easy" part. When my daily treks to a dozen doctors and specialists, labs, and imaging centers where I was poked and prodded stopped, I found myself all alone with nowhere to go, not knowing what to do, or even who to talk to. It was like being released from prison, where there was an orderly chaotic system, and then I was pushed out the door with a faint, "Good luck."

I took some time to breathe, but noticed I was holding my breath most of the time. Then, like most survivors, I tried to go back to my old life, but I had little to go back to, since I no longer had my practice. And I kept to myself, not ready to tell anyone about my cancer diagnosis. It was so personal, to say the least. And it seemed I had changed a bit, but I didn't know how. For awhile, my days were like a yo-yo. I felt good one day, ready to rejoin the living, and then the next day, I would plummet into deep depression with suicidal thoughts, where I felt exhausted and defeated, with aches and pain to accompany it all. This went on for awhile uncontrollably. I looked out the window a lot again, wished for rain, and wept profusely, day after day. There were no manuals for this.

Happiness to the Rescue!

I tried all the usual life survival methods I knew from before the cancer diagnosis, but nothing worked. The same old, same old didn't work anymore. After awhile, it dawned on me that I had to do something different, something entirely new. I couldn't go back. I could only go forward. I had to discover new tools to match my new perspective on life. But, what the heck are they and where are they hiding?!

While I was doing some research, I stumbled on the topic of happiness. I had read a few books on it. I also watched a documentary on happiness awhile back that was intriguing. But this time, for some reason, I was drawn to it like a bear to honey. I became mesmerized in a subject that rarely made an appearance in my life. After all, happiness is not what is usually associated with cancer, depression, or menopause. But I started to gobble up everything on happiness. And wouldn't you know it? Happiness was what eventually brought me back to living. *Shazam!*

It was the oddest and the most ridiculously wonderful thing. I was rescued by none other than happiness. I've discovered that happiness was not just an emotion, but a powerful tool to help me with any issue, small and big, to keep me moving, helping others, and even make my dreams come true. And, this time, I got to define what happiness was and no one else. This was my greatest discovery. Wish I knew this in kindergarten, but it's never too late.

Happiness became my survival tactic. It also gave me back hope, a will to keep living, and to seek some sanity in such perfect madness. To my surprise, happiness was easy and simple, and it felt right and natural. Thank goodness, because I can't do anything complicated any more. I've become allergic to it. Nobody needs more of that. I've also discovered that my happiness was within me and not outside of me, as I believed. So I soul-searched like mad, read everything on happiness and dove heart first into my happiness journey.

Life Experience

It turns out that my lifetime of suffering, heartbreak, disappointments, frustration, humiliation, rejection, loss, aging, bad luck, loneliness, and body parts going south, (just to mention a few) wasn't all for nothing. In fact, it gave me something amazing in return: character, life lessons to be grateful and happy, and tools to survive and thrive in my one and only life. *Wow!*

My happiness methods were eventually derived from my life experiences. *Imagine that.* I've learned that I already had the tools to make myself happy. It took some time to dig them all up. But once I did, I sorted them out, trusted my instinct, compiled life lessons and stories, and eventually, they became my happiness methods.

I practiced my set of happiness methods diligently everyday to battle all kinds of demons, and it became an unbreakable habit. To this day, these lessons help me physically, psychologically, and spiritually, and in my darkest and most frightening times. Who knew that underneath all the fears and its ugliness, I had precious tools and treasures, that were hidden inside of me, that were designed to not only help me survive life's challenges, but to help me respect, thrive, cherish, and find joy in all its mysteries.

I'm sure if you gave it some thought, you have your own set of lessons from life that can work for you, so try taking the time to learn from them. It's good to know that something precious came out of all your life and living. Nothing in your life was ever a waste. Let it pay you back twofold, at least.

Here's What I Have Learned So Far...

- Happiness is not just an emotion, but a survival tactic, and a powerful weapon and a tool.
- Happiness is within me; derived from my life experiences and from my heart and soul.
- Happiness energizes, heals, and keeps me moving, breathing, hoping & loving.
- Happiness combats daily chaos and difficult people.
- Happiness helps me achieve goals and dreams, and not the other way around.
- Life is short and unpredictable and it can change in a split second. So there's absolutely no reason to do the waiting game. I know I don't have forever.
- Waiting for happiness can be a trap and it may never come the way I imagine it. I've seen people waste their whole lives and miss out on everything waiting for happiness.
- I can always find some happiness with what I have, where I am, who I am with, and who I am right now.
- Happiness is inside of me.
- Happiness is a choice.

You definitely don't have to have a major illness or any medical or emotional issues to be happy. As a matter of fact, one of the smartest things you can do is to take preventive measures early in your life. It's never too early or too late to be healthy and happy. If it were up to me, happy would start even before birth, in your mommy's tummy and continue until your last day. Studies show that babies in the womb are affected by the mother's diet, environment, and moods. So start happy at any age or circumstances. It can happen anywhere to anyone.

The life lessons in this book are the ones I've discovered in a lifetime of living through good and bad times, and in laughter and tears, that all led to my survival and happiness. In my many perilous journeys in life, these life lessons were the reward, weapon, and gift to help me survive each and every day with whatever life throws at me, and to find happiness in it. Today, happiness is my medicine, my hope, and my purpose. It keeps me sane in an insane world.

I wanted to share my story and these life lessons to encourage you to go on a journey to seek your own set of happiness methods. I've learned the very hard way that life is fleeting. So I don't take it for granted or waste it. All we have is now. *Get it? Got it? Good!*

Welcome aboard and pat yourself on the back for having the courage to be happy, no matter who, what, or where you are.

Hold on tight. Here we go to our happy adventure!

Daily Happiness vs. Grandiose Happiness

Most people associate happiness with grandiose events, such as graduation, weddings, promotions, big breaks, having a baby, and winning the lottery, etc. But studies consistently show that the happy, euphoric feeling of special events is short-lived, fleeting, and soon forgotten. In fact, our daily happiness has the greatest impact on our lives. This makes sense, because we have more of everyday life than the huge events that occur once in awhile in our whole lifetime. For example, we only have a week or two of vacation time a year (some people don't even have that) and the rest is everyday life. Thus, we need to consciously incorporate daily habits of happiness to reap the benefits, rather than wait for the "ta-da" moments, which may or may not come. It might be a long wait, and remember, we don't do waiting any more.

Besides, if you're expecting that euphoric feeling of happiness all the time, you might explode. I'm not even sure if it's physically possible for one to be jumping up and down out of sheer happiness with the face stretched out in every direction all the time. What if it gets stuck there? *Not pretty.*

Most genuinely happy people are content, at peace, and stay relatively positive more times than not in a given day. This doesn't mean they are Buddha's cousin or a saint all the time. They are human beings and they have flare-ups and temper tantrums. They might even swear, cry, and are overwhelmed by life's unfair woes. They'll even run away and hide in a cave from time to time. And that's completely normal and okay, but the difference is they come back to life and happy relatively fast, and keep going. So being happy is not something that is a cure for all or something that can happen 24/7. That would be too much for us to expect from ourselves. We don't need more pressure in our lives of any kind. Daily happiness is about lifting some of that with a small dose of happy in our everyday lives that can subtly and quietly be extraordinary. *Capiche?*

Brain & Happiness

Did you know we can exercise brain power?
We can actually recondition our brain to create a behavior or a habit.
Cool.

According to scientists and studies, doing the same thing at the same time everyday for two to three weeks consistently can help the brain to rewire, develop a pattern, and eventually turn it into a habit to become an automatic behavior. That means we can actually influence our brain to be more positive, optimistic, and happy, keeping us healthy, active, and vital, to live a long and fulfilling life. *Sounds good to me.*

According to Harvard studies, when our brain is in the positive and happy mode, it also performs more efficiently. It's true the other way around too. When our brain is in a negative or stress mode, it will perform poorly. That makes sense too. You know you don't feel as sharp, imaginative, or productive when you are depressed, tired, and pessimistic. Same goes for the brain. It needs to be in a positive mode to increase our creativity, intelligence, productivity, energy level, (all the good stuff), which helps us achieve our goals, become satisfied and successful, and have better relationships with others. So make a conscious effort to incorporate a happy behavior, (five minutes a day to start) everyday, and it will become a habit. This is how I did it and it's second nature now. And isn't it nice to know we have some power over our own brain and behavior? And you'd thought it was the aliens. *OK, maybe...*

Benefits of Happiness

Studies consistently show there is an immediate connection between our emotions and the immune system, and being in a happy mode can help us build stronger bodies and minds, inside and out. Happiness benefits our health in every way. Here are a few examples:

- **Increases our immune system.**
  When we are in a happy, positive, and a relaxed mode, our master glands releases immune-boosting hormones, such as serotonin, dopamine, relaxin and oxytocin. When these super hormones hit our bloodstream, they send signals to our body to make more immune cells. That's like creating more soldiers in your body to fight all kinds of foreign intruders, from a cold virus to cancer cells.

- **Increases white blood cells.**
  Even five minutes of laughter a day can significantly boost the number of our natural killer cells, which is a certain type of white blood cell that could fight tumors and infected cells, among other things.

- **Helps your body and mind feel lighter and balanced.**

- **Reduces stress.**

- **Improves your temperament.**
  People don't get under your skin as much, and you are calmer and less reactive.

- **Creates a healthier state of mind overall.**

- **Give you a positive attitude.**

- **Helps you be more focused.**

- **Helps you enjoy the day and life more.**

- **Makes you feel friendlier and more willing to give, care and help.**

- **Helps you recognize the joy and the good in a day**

- **Keeps you in the present and helps you move forward.**

- **Pays it forward.**
  When people are happy, they tend to share and give more.

As you can see, happiness can affect every aspect of your body and mind in a positive way. And it doesn't take a lot to achieve a little bit of happiness in your day to make all these things happen and turn it into a habit. Soon, it will become automatic.

As you ease into implementing happiness into your daily life, you'll find more benefits and methods of your own. I hope you'll give it a try. It's bound to spread to everyone and everything around you. It's quite magical.

How to be Happy Tips
Emotional Housekeeping

The Unhappy

Before I could define my happiness, I had to first look at what was making me unhappy, because happiness can't come out when there's so much unhappiness blocking the way. That meant I had to look at some of my emotional issues, *a.k.a.* "garbage, baggage, obstacles, and crap," that were serious barricades to my happiness. Yup! It was time to identify and acknowledge the elephants, the crocodiles, and the bears in my living room. But instead of approaching it with fear and anger, I decided to sit down with them, have some coffee, and have a genuine heart-to heart-talk. Like, "Hey, Mr. Bear, what brought you here? What do you want from me? And what will help you to leave and find your own living room?" Approaching it this way made the process a lot less scary and confrontational for me. I've realized that not everything has to be a war.

Being unhappy most of the time can affect your whole being, your whole life. It can cause medical and psychological problems, unhealthy habits and negative behavior, and poor relationships with your family, partners, children, friends, pets, and others. It also sucks energy and life out of you, often disabling talent, imagination, creativity, and even compassion. Above all, your unhappiness hurts those you love the most, as you dump your misery on those closest to you, consciously or unconsciously. And your unhappy behavior can be passed onto future generations, so you need to address it as soon as you can.

Also, I've decided to accept some of my issues, which were never really gonna go away. So I've learned to manage and live with them. But this time, I got to choose how I looked at the issue and I would be in control. For example, my depression will always be with me to some degree. I've acknowledged that. So I've made peace with it, and when it comes my way for an unwelcomed visit, I know what to do. I have resources. Sometimes I even take advantage of it by using my depressive episode as a break or an opportunity to rest and just be. But still, I am in control. I will decide my response and actions. Acceptance is just as medicinal and potent. But when I have to, I will battle. No problem. But at this age and stage, I'd rather have tea and cake and chat with Mr. Elephant most of the time. It's much calmer and there are fewer casualties, dents, scars, and empty tissue boxes at the end of the day.

Reduce the Unhappy

We spend most of our days focused on all that is unhappy in our lives. It could be endless. Actually, happy is all around us. But we've been conditioned not to recognize it, so it's become invisible. Unfortunately, we are still bombarded with everything unhappy every day, all day long, by many sources like the media, work, unhappy and difficult people, control freaks, bad companies that feed off of your fear and unhappiness. And it's easy to get caught up. So we have to make a conscious effort to limit our exposure to it. This is within our power and we have to act on it.

I used to be a journalist. I was glued to the news 24/7 and that habit stayed with me long after I left the business. And I didn't even know it was affecting me. Most people don't. But eventually, I saw the world and myself in a very negative and jaded way. Eventually, that's how people defined me. Not good. So in my quest for happy, I stopped watching bad news and horrific stories as much as I can. When I do watch the news or surf the internet, I focus on positive news and stories. Sometimes, I tape the news program and then just fast forward to the good stories. I also don't read books or watch movies that are violent, depressing, traumatic, and disturbing. So many of the "entertainment" sources are. But we can block it out. Again, it's within our power to choose what we are exposed to, the unhappy or the happy. So reduce the negative exposure of every kind everyday and focus on the positive, inspirational, funny, and good stories in the world and in your own life. They may not be in the spotlight all the time, but they are out there. We just haven't looked.

Steps to Deal with the Unhappy

- Identify and acknowledge the "unhappy" in your life: Things, places, people, etc.

- What/who triggers your unhappiness?

- Avoid, reduce, and eliminate unhappy things.

- Avoid and/or disconnect with unhappy, toxic people.

- Avoid negative news, bad and sad stories.

Most news is about crimes, murder, natural disasters, war, diseases, corruption, politics, and bad people getting rich. *Depressing.* These are things we don't have too much control over, so being upset about it won't benefit anyone. It might even work against you, because when you're upset, you could be physically and emotionally immobile and ineffective. That won't help anyone, including yourself. So limit your exposure and focus on what you can control, and positive actions and results.

- Break the cycle of automatically tuning into negative resources out of habit every day.

- Stay away from negative, violent, dark, and traumatic and disturbing movies, shows, books, photos. Focus mainly on positive and inspirational materials.

- Try to take calls from mostly positive people. No more whiners and complainers. Thank you!

- Avoid self-defeating behaviors such a overeating, drug & alcohol abuse, compulsive shopping, and others.

- Release and process your unhappy issues in a safe and trusting environment. Psychotherapy is always a good option. But you can always talk to someone you trust and who actively listens.

- Expression Therapy: Not everybody is comfortable with talk therapy. There are numerous ways to express one's unhappiness: art, dance, writing, and laugh therapy, just to mention a few. Explore the methods, that interests you.

- Exercise: One of the best ways to release all kinds of unhappy and toxins in your body and mind is to move. Whether it's a brisk walk or an intense Zumba class, sweat out all the unhappy. It feels incredible.

- The Punching Bag. You can get one of those punching/boxing bags and punch away. Sometimes, I put a picture or the name of the person who is making me unhappy and let it rip. Often, it's myself, as I get on my own nerves. It's very therapeutic and affordable. You can also use pillows. You can punch and scream into them. I'm sure you've seen this in the movies.

Seek Out and Increase Happy

While you are reducing the unhappy in your day, you also need to increase your happy exposure. On a daily basis, I seek out websites, literature, TV shows, people, and places that are positive and happy. It's out there for us to grab and swallow. I couldn't see it before. But now, my lenses are clear and I let it all soak into my skin, heart, psyche, and soul. *Love that feeling!*

Start with just five minutes a day to seek out happy things and people, and it will make you feel different, even though the world is the same. It's more powerful than you can imagine and it changes your attitude, your work, and your life. And it spreads to others, as it can change the world little bit at a time. It still blows my mind. Our happiness can have a positive effect on the whole world. *Awesome!* When you are happy, you make healthy and happy choices that can fight all kind of causes for the human race, animals, and mother earth. It's the win-win all around.

Discover Your Own Combination

I love combos, especially at restaurants. Don't you? You get to eat a variety of foods, and taste different things all at once, and it's usually more affordable. So it goes for happiness. We can't survive on just one thing or one person in life. We all need a combination of things and people to make us happy. Can you imagine eating just one thing or being with just one person all the time for the rest of your life? *Yikes!* To be happy, we need different interests, as well as different people, to make us feel secure, calm, and joyous. Everybody is unique. So, find your own combination of things that make you happy and let it evolve with time, life experience, and age.

Happy is an Inside-Out Deal

A lot of people believe that tangible things like cash, cars, homes, jewelry, fancy clothes, beautiful young people, and other stuff will bring happiness. Money is always on the top of the heap. But studies show that money doesn't make people happier. Wealthy people are not the happiest people on earth. Even most lottery winners say money has made their lives worse. Money often comes with human vultures, greed, and a lot of uninvited guests that want a piece of your fortune.

According to studies, once people have their basic needs meet, like shelter, food and clothing; higher income does not bring more happiness. As a matter of fact, there's not much happiness level difference between someone who makes $5,000 or $50,000 a month. Interesting, don't you think? Sadly, a lot of people still believe in the formula: *Money =happiness*. A lot of people waste their whole lives chasing after money and miss out on their own children's lives and dreams. Now, that's tragic.

Some people also think fame will bring happiness. Count how many celebrities and public figures you think are happy. Then count all the ones that seem quite miserable. Think of all the child stars. How many didn't have a tragic ending? Sad in many ways. I've interviewed many famous people as a journalist, and most of them said fame is neither glamorous nor a major factor in happiness. But then the starry eyes of those seeking fame and fortune all over the world want to find that out on their own.

I've learned the hard and long way that no partner, money, position, or thing outside of me will make me happy most of the time. The truth is that if I am happy and I like myself and my life, things fall into place. It may not be the way I imagined, but different, more creative, and sometimes more suitable to my existence. When I am content and at peace, I've found that I don't need a lot of stuff, superficial stuff, to define myself and my happiness.

Relying too much on anything or anyone to bring you happiness can create a dangerous dependency. Only you can define your happiness now and always. You are the one person who does not leave you.

Happy Starts with You

I've heard somebody say, "High school is never over." It certainly feels true sometimes, doesn't it? It's amazing how much time, energy, money, and life we spend just to get someone else's approval, validation, and to get into the "in crowd." And I'm not just talking about high school. Grown-ups are still at it. To some degree, we need other's validation, but it's exhausting, and at times at great expense, and it doesn't always work, and often not worth the degradation.

We seek validation from our family, friends, bosses, coworkers, neighbors, and strangers, and just about everybody else, and yet, we rarely reach out or spend any time to get the approval of the most important person, who is with you every single second of the day from birth to death. It took me half a century, but I've realized that the only person's approval I need is my own, at least to start with. Once I'm good with myself, it seems others are as well. Less work and -- you guessed it -- I'm happier.

How to Start

Find some time, preferably alone, in a quiet place without any distraction. Jot down a few things that made you happy in the past and present. Go down memory lane and think of what made you happy and why. Let it come to your mind easily, and give it a go.

Keep an Open Mind and Try New Things That Intrigue You.

Your daily happy methods should be like eating, breathing, and sleeping, and on your "to do" list. It's that important and it works in a subtle and yet powerful way. Like anything in life, the more you do it, the easier and more habitual it becomes. Same goes for happy. I have happy projects that are easy and challenging, and I enjoy them both immensely. It makes me happy, both the journey and the results. So, rocket science can be somebody's happiness.

Keep it Simple, at Least to Start With.

Go swing on a swing. Have a chocolate cake with a friend. Go see your favorite movie, skip around the block or around the house, sing in the shower again, pick up an old hobby, go fly a kite, stare at the stars outside, lie on the grass and look up at the blue sky or the stars, play with your dogs, cows, and hamsters, learn to cha cha, volunteer at an animal rescue, laugh for no reason, *etc.* Remember, YOU get to decide. We've already had too many people tell us who and what we should be our whole lives. This time, you define your own happiness.

Keep it Practical and Doable.

It doesn't have to be grand or involve your entire life savings or risking your life. The best way to start is to incorporate happy methods five minutes a day into your existing lifestyle and go from there. If you can do more, great!

Find Your Own Definition of Happiness.

For the first time in my life, I've decided to define what happiness was for myself. I am a firm believer that people should define their own happiness and not accept someone else's definition. People can offer help and make suggestions, but you have the final word. It's your life and you know what makes you happy. If you don't, it's time to find out.

You can certainly read more about happiness to get some ideas, and learn about different theoretical perspectives and the science behind it. There are a lot of fascinating studies and results about happiness in general and about positive psychology. Explore at your own pace, but don't forget to reach into yourself to find most of the answers.

Don't Obsess Over Happiness.

Don't become obsessed by spending all your waking hours on the internet or otherwise looking for happiness. That's not what it's about. Go about your business, your day, your life, and incorporate some happy things, simply and naturally. Like I've said, start with just five minutes a day with activities that make you happy and give you joy. Also, diversify your sources and go at your own pace.

Start and End the Day with Happy Things.

I start and end the day with happy and positive things, places, and people. You'll have a better day, fewer nightmares, and happier dreams. I never walk out the door in the morning in a negative mood. I'll create a positive situation, even if it's just saying out loud that I have a lot to look forward to and I am going to approach it all with a good and happy attitude. I also don't go to bed in a bad mood. I'll take the time to put myself in a happy mode. I usually meditate and/or watch something funny on TV, read inspirational stories, or get wonderful hugs from my family, or simply smile and say, "I did all right today. I'm doing good." You can find your own unique ways.

Take Action!

Nothing happens without action, at least not for most people. Once I got my set of happy methods that appealed to me and were doable, I set up a daily action plan to implement them. And it wasn't hard. Are you kidding? I couldn't wait to get to them first thing in the morning, throughout the day, at nights, weekends, and holidays. Why, because I wanted to be happy. What else? This isn't rocket science. And happy acts are usually simple and easy things you can do every day, that doesn't require a lot of time or energy unless you want it to.

Remember, you don't need to invest a lot of time or money, or turn your life upside down. The point is to incorporate happiness in your existing life a little bit at a time, as you work towards your goals and dreams.

So put it on your to-do list, get out of your head, and JUST DO IT!

Cardinal Rule of Happiness

Make sure your happiness does not harm you or anyone else.
Happy acts should never hurt anyone or anything.

Happy Life Lessons

These are my life lessons that taught me how to be happy so far

You Gotta Laugh!

"A day without laughter is a day wasted."
Charlie Chaplin

Mary had two choices for a date on her 42nd birthday. Winston was a forty something, muscle-bulging, tall, drop-dead gorgeous guy with dark wavy hair, beautiful skin, an intoxicating smile, and plump lips beckoning for a kiss. However, Winston did not have an ounce of sense of humor. He didn't find anything funny. He didn't even see the point of laughing. He said, "It messes up my face." It messes up your face?! *Oh my.*

Eddie was in his 50s, slightly balding with a protruding belly. He was also two inches shorter than Mary and quite colorblind with his outfits. But the minute he walked in the door, Eddie lit up the room. He was funny, funny, funny! He had a great sense of humor - and he didn't have trouble making fun of his hair, his belly, or his height. He laughed all the time, at himself and with others. He made everybody laugh, especially Mary.

Mary fell madly in love with Eddie. Every time he made her laugh, she wanted to lunge across the room and rip his shirt off. A sense of humor is that powerful, sexy, and contagious. Poor Winston stayed home analyzing in writing why Mary turned him down. He scratched his wavy hair a lot, but he couldn't find any answers. After all, he was Mr. Wonderful. So he went for a facial. Eddie on the other hand got very, very lucky with Mary. They got married a year later and they are still laughing today.

Did you laugh today? I mean really laugh?
I've discovered that a sense of humor and laughing are sheer survival tools, to combat everything from the daily madness to overwhelmingly painful events in our lives. It's what keeps us sane in an absolutely insane world. Imagine what your life would be without laughter. I bet you could use more of it.

As people grow older, they seem to laugh less. When we were kids, we laughed all the time for no particular reason. Now, we need it more than ever. A great sense of humor and laughing are what will keep you looking and feeling young. There's nothing more beautiful than a person who throws his or her head back and roar with laughter. I love it. It's contagious and intoxicating, and incredibly therapeutic.

Never lose your sense of humor, especially as you grow older. The happiest people on the planet are the ones who are able to laugh at themselves and life. And these people are not necessarily well off. On the contrary, they have their own set of troubles, sad stories, and challenges. But instead of frowning about them, they laugh about them. A sense of humor gives them the strength to carry on with life's inescapable burdens.

Abraham Lincoln had a great sense of humor, even though he had a very difficult life. He had a string of defeats in politics, failed in business, and suffered from depression. And, sadly, his one true love, as well as his son, died young. On top of everything, his pants were flooding all the time. Lincoln was unusually tall for his generation and very poor, so the hand-me-downs from his neighbors were a few sizes too small. *Embarassing.* When he became president, someone called Lincoln "two-faced." To that he replied, *"If I was two-faced, would I be wearing this one?"* During the Civil War, someone asked him how he could possible joke and laugh in the midst of all the misery the war brought. He said, "I laugh because I must not cry." Mr. Lincoln laughed often. Otherwise, he couldn't have endured the atrocities of war and so much more.

There's a lot of scientific evidence now that prove humor is one of the most effective treatments around. It's medicinal. It may not show on X-rays or CAT scans, but humor can temporarily cure just about anything that life throws at you.

As a matter of fact, many hospitals have patients watching "The Three Stooges," "I Love Lucy," "Laurel and Hardy," and others funnies to alleviate their ailments. So laugh as much as you can every day. At least five minutes. Put it on your "to do" list. It's a must.

Remember, if you can find humor in your life or anything else for that matter, you've conquered it. So go ahead. Open your mouth real wide, hold onto your tummy, and let it rip!

Health
It Really is Everything!

> *"If you don't take care of your body,*
> *where are you going to live?"*
> *Unknown*

With depression, cancer, menopause, and other ailments that are popping up with aging, I take my health very seriously and never take it for granted. I've gone to hell and back and I've seen and felt firsthand, the pain and the nightmares, of both the body and the mind. Although it took awhile, I've learned that I am ultimately in control of my health.

When I went for my physical, Helen, the nurse, asked me the usual questions. She asked me what medications I was on and if I'd like a piece of paper to write them down. I said, "I'm not on any medication." Helen froze. All things in her station stopped. She looked at my chart vigorously and said, "That can't be. You're over 40. There has to be some error somewhere." She shook her head in disbelief and amazement. She said I was the first person over 40 not on any medication. For some reason, that did not comfort me.

At a restaurant, I heard a happy couple say, "Health is everything. Without health, we have nothing." And with every glass of wine, we proudly toast to, "A votre santé!" We say it and we hear it, but most of us don't do it. We don't exercise health, as we should, as we need to. Whether we're at midlife or not, we have to focus on our health or we will lose it. It's that simple. Being old and sick is something we have the power to prevent to some degree. That means health has to move up to number one on our priority and to-do list. And this time, health is not just about our external body. It's the care and the balance of our whole being, which includes our body, mind, and soul. Be good to it all and it will carry us well until our next journey.

Most people consider their body growing old and sagging as one of the major depressors of midlife. Who can blame them? It's reality. You can see it happening before your very eyes, and it ain't pretty. However, while the external body may grow "mature," the inner body is just awakening and ready to blossom, if you let it. The inner body is born and it grows to make you stronger, deeper, and wiser. And it never wrinkles or sags. *Yes!*

How you take care of your body and mind now can greatly influence the length and the quality for the rest of your life, as well as how good and bad you will look and feel every day. There's more information about taking care of your health today than ever before in the history of human existence. You have absolutely no excuse. Health, inside and out, is in your control. What you do or don't do is up to you. If this isn't getting through, go to the nearest hospital. It will be a loud wake-up call.

Here Are Some Suggestions to Start Your Health Journey:
Make sure you check with your doctor before incorporating these methods or any changes in your diet or physical activity.

Eat Healthy

That means eating foods we human beings were designed to eat to survive and be healthy. Eat mostly real food such as vegetables, fruits, grains, and nuts, and avoid processed and fast foods, and white sugar, bread, and pasta. Also reduce or eliminate eating meat and dairy, and drinking, soda, alcohol and caffeine. Processed deli meats have been linked to heart disease to cancer. Avoid GMO and non organic foods, as they are laced with pesticides, additives, and preservatives that can cause havoc in your body and affect your moods, as well as pollute our environment. Always read the food information and ingredients on the back of the product you are buying. You have an enormous power through your food choices to be healthy, and save money, as well as protect our food source, clean water, wildlife and earth. Imagine that.

Exercise Regularly

Our bodies are designed to move. So exercise regularly, at least 30 minutes of aerobic workout, 5 times a week. It can be as easy as brisk walking or dancing in your room. No need to get fancy. Do what you enjoy and you'll keep at it longer. If you don't like exercising alone or need some motivation, you can also workout with a friend, take a sports, yoga, or dance class, or even join a walking community. And dogs love walks too!

Stop Smoking, Excessive Alcohol & Caffeine Consumption, and Doing Drugs

There is absolutely no reason to smoke any more. We know the facts and the truths. It kills one out of 5 people. Second hand smoke also kills. A colleague who allowed his patients to smoke in therapy sessions died of lung cancer. He never smoked a day in his life.

Excessive drinking can lead to anemia, cancer, cardiovascular disease, dementia, infectious disease, depression, and nerve damage, just to mention a few. It can also destroy relationships, families, and dreams. And often, children adopt excessive drinking through learned behavior and it gets passed on. There's a lot more danger and horror than most people realize. So, address the issue before it gets out of control.

A lot of people don't realize they can be addicted to caffeine. It's the most commonly used mood altering, legal drug around the globe, as 90% of adults and children consume it every day. And, just because it's legal doesn't mean it cannot be addictive. There are things in the drug stores that people have become addicted to. Caffeine is in a lot of things such as coffee, tea, sodas, chocolate, and even some gums. So exercise moderation. Check with your doctor to see how much is reasonable for your health.

If you are serious about being healthy, not being a burden to your family or anyone else, and improving the quality of your life, you need to face up to your drug habits and addiction of every kind. Prevent and stop before it becomes a dependency. A 100 people die from drug addiction every day alone, but you don't have to fight these battles alone. There are plenty of help available. The first step is your determination.

Practice Preventive Medicine

That means you have to go see your doctor at least once a year like clockwork for your physical exams and do necessary preventive tests, such as mammograms, endoscopies, colonoscopies, blood work, etc. Depending on your medical history, the doctors should make recommendations accordingly. Don't wait around until you have aches, pains, and bumps. There are too many tragic and fatal stories of people who waited too long and it was all too late. Many diseases and disorders can be prevented, and symptoms can be managed or greatly reduced with preventive care.

Become Familiar with Your Family Medical History

This is crucial in knowing what to expect, especially in the second half of your life. Many diseases and mental disorders are hereditary, like some cancers and diabetes, as well as depression to schizophrenia, just to mention a few. So ask your parents, aunts, uncles, and everyone else related to you and do screenings to prevent diseases proactively. Don't ever wait until you see or feel a symptom. It may be too late.

Manage Your Stress

We know by now that stress is the number one killer in America. In order to manage stress, you have to work on your body and mind, as well as discover the sources of your stress. Why are you excessively drinking, eating, yelling, and smoking? Why are you sleeping too much or not at all or having nightmares? Go and find out what is bugging you psychologically and emotionally. This can affect your health, and your relationships, professionally and personally.

Make an effort to reduce the negatives in your life such as things, places, and even people. At the same time, increase the positives by incorporating more laughter, good people, joy, hobbies, and happiness on a daily basis. It's already there in your life. You just haven't looked in that direction. You may not be able to avoid all the negatives, but you have the power to change how you look at it.

I would recommend psychotherapy for everyone. It's not just about dealing with mental disorders, but about confronting, coping, and making peace with yourself and your issues, not to mention venting all your frustration in a safe place. And the more you know about yourself, the more empowered you will be to take good care of yourself and those you truly love. Develop a plan to always combat stress through healthy eating, exercising, laughing, relaxing, and finding the time to calm your body and mind. The choice is up to you.

Get Your Medical Team Together

Start by taking the time and energy to put together your medical team, consisting of a general practitioner, internist, optometrist, dentist, gynecologist (for women), and other specialists you require. Make sure your doctors are both competent and caring. Do some research and legwork on the physicians and make sure they are credible in every way. As you grow older, your medical team will be crucial in keeping you well all around.

On Medication

As we grow older, there's a chance we might be taking some kind of medication. So educate yourself. Research the drugs you are taking and ask your doctors lots of questions, and monitor your body's reaction to the drugs, and inquire about alternative, natural, and non-drug treatment options as well. Healthy eating, exercising, and stress management have reduced and eliminated a dependency on pills for many people young or older. No one knows your body better than you do. So listen to it. Consult with your physician and NEVER EVER assume anything! I want you to be around for a long time.

Weight & Diet

I have to say a few words on weight gain and diet because the whole world is obsessed with being thin. And we are losing the real perspective on health. Being thin is not more important than being healthy. Let me say that again: BEING THIN IS NOT MORE IMPORTANT THAN BEING HEALTHY!! Health is always #1. This applies to people of all ages, by the way. If you don't have a body to stand on, you won't even have a chance to be thin or gorgeous. Remember that. Write it down and post it somewhere.

As a woman, I have at times succumbed to the whole obsession of being thin and attractive. But I've discovered the truth about weight and beauty. If you want to lose weight, eat healthy and exercise and the weight will automatically come off. Then, you will discover your true body image that belongs to you and only you, rather than someone else. There's only one unique body like yours. So, don't deny yourself. Don't you want to know what that looks like? I do. It's one of a kind and pure beauty.

Diets have never worked, and they're expensive, stressful, and ridiculous. Why allow strangers, models, celebrities, and people who don't know you define your body image? It's such an insult to yourself. Eat healthy, healing, delicious food, exercise, and face your emotional issues, and you'll not only be healthy and confident, but happy all around.

For years, I was a night eater. Come 8 o' clock and I had to fight myself from going into the kitchen and swallowing the refrigerator. Sometimes, I would eat past midnight or even in the middle of the night. I knew it was emotional eating. Often, I was bored, anxious, stressed, lonely, and depressed: all great reasons to stuff my poor body with food, bad food, to give me instant gratification and a complete distraction to avoid my miserable reality. Of course, the consequences were huge. I mean literally. I woke up with an extra thigh or butt in the morning, not to mention all the health issues like digestive problems, bloating, constipation, weight gain, lethargy, just to mention a few. And it was a cycle. Looking and feeling bad led me to do, what else, but stuff myself again. It was only when I started eating healthy and working on my issues in therapy that I stopped overeating and being a night eater. *Thank goodness.* It was costing me in many ways.

I strongly recommend facing your psychological or emotional issues attached to weight gain. Often a lack of self-esteem or control plays a major role in overeating and distorted body image. You're not alone. Most people with a weight problem have emotional issues. But it won't go away unless you face them. You won't have to do it alone and you have the courage to do it.

We think about health only when we get sick or when we start to grow old. But health should be something we think and act on from childhood to old age. Because when you are healthy, you can do anything, be anyone, and provide security for yourself and those you love, and thrive without pain and pills. Health is truly the greatest gift you can give to yourself and those you love. There's nothing like it. And it's much easier to be happy when you are healthy than screaming in pain.

If you feel you don't have time to take care of your health, think of all the people you will hurt when you are sick or dying. Do you want to inflict that kind of pain and burden on those you cherish? You are smart and old enough to get it. Seriously, no more excuses. Health cannot be put on hold.

Take good care of your body and mind. It's the only one you've got and it's working hard for you every second of the day. It's a tough job, so don't burden it with all kind of poison and toxins. Be good to it by giving all the amunition it needs, such as powerful food, exercise to move things along, and reduce stress and increase happiness, so your body can fight to keep you alive and well.

Health will be the best investment of your life. Here's to your health my friend!

Ah...Food
Eat Healthy to be Happy

*"There is no sincerer love
than the love of food."*
George Bernard Shaw

Thank God for food, *seriously.*

It may be the greatest invention of the gods. It's certainly the most reliable reward for us poor human beings, who have to deal with insanity, chaos, and injustice every single freakin' day. And hands down, food is one of the greatest, if not THE greatest, pleasures in life. Ask any female on the planet. Food is also one of the best antidotes to life. When all else fails, we have food. When all is well, we have food. *Yippee!* We work hard every day so we can get together with family and friends to chow down. This is universal. This is what we all want and need. My daily goal is to EAT! There are no better words in any language than, *"Breakfast, lunch, dinner, snack, chocolate cake, and let's eat!"* And let me tell you, food gets better with age.

Food is life, literally.

I've learned that if you eat healthy, as we were meant to via nature, it will nourish our body, mind, and spirit. You will not only be healthy, you'll shed the unwanted weight, increase your longevity, reduce painful symptoms, prevent diseases, heal faster, and be ultimately happier. Food is medicinal, pleasurable, creative, and of course, insanely yummy! Is there anything better, I ask you?

What we eat affects us physically and emotionally. When we do food right by selecting healthy meals, exercising balance and moderation, and planning carefully, as well as educate ourselves about basic nutrition, food is probably the best medicine around.

Managing your own food and diet will also help prevent waste and save you money tremendously. When you decide to treat your body better, it naturally does good things back for you, your family, and the whole planet. *Awesome!*

I incorporate healthy/natural foods in my daily diet. It's automatic now. It's not hard nor is it a sacrifice. On the contrary, you will be introduced to nature's finest dining for your palate and pleasure. The possibilities are endless. And while you are enjoying clean, pure, luscious healthy foods, they will be preventing, fighting, curing, healing, rebuilding, and energizing your whole being to keep you alive to keep living.

Keep It Simple

You don't have to change your whole diet all at once or turn your life upside down. That could be a set up for failure and frustration. Keep things simple. Incorporate more organic vegetables and fruits in one of your meals a day. Go meatless on Mondays. Chew more times before swallowing your food. Try using smaller plates to hold your meal. Drink more water than sodas throughout the day. Rely on nature and eat food you know are real. Take baby steps. Like the tortoise in "Tortoise and the Hare," Go nice and slow and you'll not only win the race, but live a long, happy life.

Reduce or Eliminate Dairy and Meat

Most animal products are filled with antibiotics, hormones, steroids, and fillers and the animals are fed GMO grain and corn, which are not their natural diet. All this gets passed onto us and thus it creates all kind of health issues from allergies, heart disease, to cancer. Also, the poor animals are treated cruelly, confined to dark and tight spaces, rarely sees sun or outdoors, or ever stand on natural ground their whole lives. And sadly, the calves are never fed their own mother's milk and denied contact, as they are fed synthetic food, just until they are big enough to slaughter.

A lot of people think they need to drink milk or eat meat for protein. It's one of the greatest myths around. You can get more protein through vegetables and other natural sources. And by the way, U.S. has not had a protein deficiency case since the 1940's.

According to the World Health Organization and others, processed meat causes cancer and red meat will probably cause cancer. And the healthiest, happiest, and the longest living people on the planet don't consume meat, or eat it only on special occasions, sparingly. If you must consume meat or while you are tapering off, try to consume organic, pasture and humanely raised, grass fed meat. It makes a difference in your health every way. I hope you at least try going meatless in the near future. It has saved many lives, young and old. Start with incorporating meatless mondays for yourself and your family. You'll never know until you try it. Find out for yourself.

The United Nations, numerous scientists, and others have reported repeatedly that more than 51% of greenhouse emission, climate change is caused by animal agriculture, affecting our land, ocean, and air. It is also the number one cause of water pollution. A person going meatless or reducing meat can save earth from global warming and toxic pollution more than any single act.

About Chickens & Eggs

Sadly, all those labels on eggs mean very little at the grocery store. So, I found another way. Keep chickens.

Some of the happiest people I know have chickens. I know that sounds funny, but chickens are smart, incredible, and so much fun. Both the grownups and the kids love it. Chickens have amazing and distinct personalities. And by the way, chickens are not vegetarians. They thrive on insects as well as veggies. And it's a wonderful circle of life in our own backyard. We feed them kitchen scraps, they eat the bugs (solving the bug problems), and their poop becomes a natural fertilizer, which we used for our garden, that makes our veggies, fruits, and herbs grow, and so on. There's absolutely no waste in nature.

Many cities allow people to raise chickens in backyards, so check it out. They also give out compost bins for free or at a very low price. Ever since I've had eggs from home raised chickens, I cannot eat any other kind. They are fresh, natural, tasty, and downright beautiful.

On several occasions, I visited commercial chicken and egg factories and I've always ended up vomiting and having nightmares. If I told you how they are treated, what they are fed, you wouldn't be able to eat them or have a descent night's sleep.

Can't keep chickens? No problem. Find people who do. That's how I got started. I bet there are people in your community raising chickens and they would be very happy to share, educate, and even exchange their eggs for something you can donate, make or bake. You'll not only get fresh eggs and meet chickens, but build communities and friendships. Priceless.

Learn to Grow Your Own Food to Some Degree

Nowadays, you don't even need a yard. People grow things everywhere from pots, containers, raised beds, walls, rooftops, and even pouches. There are also community gardens where you can grow and share the harvest. How fun is that? And there's something so gratifying and spiritual about growing and eating your own food straight from earth. It's also great exercise, and an amazing experience, and I want you to experience it firsthand. It's good for your body and soul.

Buy Seasonal, Local, and Diversify

So many people are a creature of habit and only shop for their food in one store every week. There are a plethora of food sources, including the farmers market, ethnic and specialty stores, farm stands, and even online. Also, check out seasonal veggies and fruits. They are abundant, fresh, affordable, and absolutely delicious. I even visit some local farms and pick the foods myself. There's nothing like food right from the vines. Sometimes I eat as I pick and hang on a tree. So much fun!

Some people only use salt and pepper for their spices, when there is a plethora of spices available to us, such as tumeric, cumin, chili powder, smoked paprika, etc. Instead of using salt to enhace your food, try different spices and herbs, instead. They are healthier than salt, incredibly diverse, and it will be a culinary adveture, full of delious foods that will lead to your health and a happy dance. Great food has a tendency to do that.

Exercise Moderation

Don't do extremes. They don't work. Exercise moderation and enjoy your favorite foods from time to time. For example, I love french fries, but the conventional form is deep fried in horrible fat and doused with processed salt. So, I often seek a healthier, alternative option such as baking or using healthy/alternative oil, and use spices such as smoked paprika or cumin, or sea salt. You can always turn any "unhealthy" food into a healthy one. It's delicious and there are no unhealthy consequences. It's a win-win. Try it.

It's Impossible To Be Healthy On a Sick Planet

Sadly, our majestic planet Earth, our one and only home and food source, is plagued with pollution and toxins caused by man on a monumental scale. Our food supply is in peril as our soil, water, and air is contaminated with pesticides, carbon monoxide, and harmful chemicals, which creates diseases, killing people, animals and nature. For example, we depend on bees to provide for 30% of our food and 90% for wildlife plants, and man is killing them at an alarming rate. They are about to go extinct. We are destroying our own food supply and thus our health and ourselves.

However, as consumers we have the ultimate power to heal our planet, go above and beyond politics and ignorance, and save our source of food, and recover our health. In doing so, we can make a difference and save mother Earth for ourselves and the future generations. And it's simple and you don't even have to do anything extraordinary, and it will save you money.

It's called spending power and each and one of us has it. Every single thing you buy, whether it's a cup of coffee or a car, you are exercising your power and giving it a voice. When you buy and eat real, natural, whole foods, you are not only strengthening your body and mind, but also preventing pollution, keeping our air, water, and oceans clean, and saving our planet for us, our children, and wildlife. Just imagine if we all did this together every day. It's up to us. We have a choice.

We spend more money buying food on a daily basis than on anything else. So this can have a huge impact if we all do this together. As health-conscious, savvy shoppers, we as a group cannot be manipulated so easily by greedy, unethical companies, which are ruining our health and planet for profit.

We cannot be healthy on a sick planet. Our daily choices for what we eat can be the difference between life and death. We have a fundamental right to clean water and real food. Don't let anyone take that away from us. Remember, we have the ultimate power. Don't give it up.

Healthy delicious food = Happiness!!!

A Neurotic Midlife Crisis
Is There Any Other Kind?

"Youth is a gift of nature,
but age is a work of art."
Garson Kanin

It came around much faster than I imagined. I swear I thought I'd be younger a little longer. Didn't you? I turned 40 and WHAM! I was middle-aged. *Ughhh.*

You know what I'm talking about.Your hair's missing in action, your belly bulges and hangs for no reason, your skin feels like your wallet, your body parts are heading south, your metabolism is hitting the brakes, and you need a map to find your breasts! You don't know your spouse any more or you're called a "divorcee," and you want to return the two purple-headed kids from outer space. And by the way, what the heck happened to Prince Charming? Couldn't ask for directions?! You'd rather hang out with your dog than go into the office, and you've been thinking about quitting your job and becoming a lounge singer in Vegas, seriously! You daydream about swimming with the dolphins, sipping margaritas, and making love with a gorgeous waiter on a warm, sandy beach. On the guy side, you want to pierce your ears, buy a sports car, hit the road blasting rock n' roll, and toss the cell phone out the window, screaming "Goodbye Charlie!"You want to put on a pair of shorts and hang ten. Remember? *Oh yeah.*

All of a sudden you have gray hair protruding all over your head and you buy hair color by the truck load and cry all night long watching "Casablanca." As a matter of fact, almost everything makes you cry. What up?! The routines of your life, which had sustained you for decades, are of no comfort. You sit for hours staring out the window or at the blank wall asking yourself over and over, "IS THIS ALL THERE IS TO LIFE, TO MY LIFE?" And what will you do now that you're aging faster than the organic broccoli in the refrigerator? You're no longer the youngest one in the crowd. Death, which had been someone else's problem, is now lurking over your shoulder from an uncomfortable distance, letting you know it has arrived. You can feel your mortality. It's as subtle as a pile of bricks landing on your face. It's like one day we were young and perky, full of life and hope, and then Bam! We have aches and pain all over our bodies without even moving. Age spots seems to appear out of nowhere, and we find ourselves sitting around saying things we never said before, like, "I want to go home and lie down."What?! Sit down. Say hello to your midlife crisis.

I'm not sure what came first, the physical or the emotional crisis. But it seems they like to travel close together. We can't help it. It's like a built-in alarm clock. The minute we reach our 40s, we hear a voice from within asking annoying little midlife questions like, "What happened to my life? When did I get old? Where did my hair go? Happy New Year? I'm one year older and getting closer to death and you're wishing me a Happy New Year?!Bug off!!""Good Morning? What's the hell is good about it?" *Lovely.*

Around midlife, each of us gets a call. For some it's loud, for others it's quiet. But it's a call, an invisible inner call, which keeps on bugging us. At first, we have no idea where the call is coming from, what it is, what it wants, or how to make it go away. But it won't go away. And as human behavior goes, what we cannot understand, we try everything to dismiss, or we ignore it altogether and pretend it's not there. Denial. We try to bury it, hide it, or drown it under a lot of work, food, alcohol, and people, but it still won't go away.The more we fight the natural course of life, the harder it is. No one wins a battle with Mother Nature. The only way to make your midlife call "go away" is to answer it. And guess what? The call is coming from YOU.*Yup.* Sneaky little devil!

Nothing really happens overnight, *you know?* Your midlife was long in the making. It's actually a part of natural human development and it has a real purpose. The midlife call is to wake you up for your real true life. Yes, your real life!! So, wake up Cinderellas and Cinderfellas!! It's time to live as you were meant to; the way we want to.

It's actually quite amazing the way we human beings are designed. At midlife, the transition to the next phase of your life development kicks in. It's our second adolescence. And just like the first one, it's filled with confusion, resistance, rebellion, mystery, chaos, fear, and a lot of growing pain. But it also has excitement, adventure, and rewards that are deeper, soulful, and everlasting. And we don't have to deal with pimples, braces, acne, or be a rebel without a cause. We are going from adulthood to old age, for the lack of a better term. Midlife crisis - it's completely normal, necessary, and natural. We are growing up again. Subtle or not, we cannot escape change. It's constant throughout our lives.

I personally don't like the term "Midlife Crisis." If you look at it like a crisis, it will be. It's more of a journey; a quest or a self-discovery trip to YOU. I bet you don't know there lies within you infinite treasures that you can't even imagine. This is your ultimate reward for having survived the chaotic first half of your life. *You did it!* Now, you get to discover all the inner beauty and strength in yourself, which will help you deal with all the mystery of the second half of your life. This time it's not about work, titles, suits, or money. It's about things that truly matter, such as family, friendship, imagination, laugher, soul mates, dreams, and fun, which includes eating and dancing. *Hooray!*

Not everyone can face their midlife call and go on a self-discovery journey. It takes enormous courage to look honestly at yourself and welcome change and truly grow. A midlife call beckons those with a deep, sensitive, spiritual soul and a pure heart. After all, why are we here on earth? Do you know why you're here? It's time to find out.

By the way, we didn't get older for nothing. We learned a lot about life, survival, and relationships of all kinds. In our 40 plus years, we earned each one of our life lessons through heartache, sacrifices, breakups, risks, making fools of ourselves, unavoidable failures, disappointments, buried hopes, unrelenting sadness, broken promises, and trying everything crazy at least once. None of it was wasted. We gained our most precious asset: *life experience.* And this will guide us through our second half, our best half, where we will use what we've learned to create a brilliant life. We've grown up and now we can finally go back to playing. Midlife is a friendly reminder that we need to be truly alive in order to live. Don't stay enslaved to a desk, paperwork, and the mundane routine of your life working, paying bills, and watching TV. Before you know it, it will all be over. And you will have missed out on living.

Midlife is our second chance to get it right and it's finally our turn to live and enjoy all that we have earned and learned in forty-plus years of living. Don't forget that. The kids are finally out of the house. We don't have to listen to our parents any more or do homework. We know how things work now. We know how to get from A to B. *Finally.*

This is the real beginning, our beginning. We don't have to go through life confused, bewildered, befuddled, or stupid any more. We are now veterans and pros at it, and we know the rules of the game. We know how to use our brains. We know how to use the DVD player. We know what really matters. And now, we are going to use it all to discover our true selves, purpose, meaning, and enlightenment. We're also going to let our talents, skills, and compassion make a difference in somebody's life and our beautiful and majestic planet, which is in peril. But we can fix it with our knowhow and compassion. And finally, we are going to make love from the soul. In other words, we are going to have the time of our lives!!!

So don't wallow around feeling sorry for yourself, being obsessed with youth and sagging body parts. It's an insult to you, not to mention a colossal waste of your precious time, energy, and life. We've done enough of that already. And for heaven's sake, don't get stuck living inside your head or overanalyzing the midlife blues, or anything else for that matter. Float, coast, relax, and chill once in awhile, and take a breather and simply enjoy the natural gifts and beauty that are already in and around you. Allow yourself to see your own possibilities in the second and the best half of your life. There's still a lot of living, your best living to do. So, c'mon!

Remember, a midlife crisis is absolutely normal. What you are feeling, as annoying, confusing, and frightening as it may be, is absolutely natural. It's a journey into the next phase of our human existence. As long as you don't deny yourself the spiritual and emotional adventure to uncover the plethora of gems in your whole being, you'll be all right.

Life, time, and age has given us a gift. Let's open it, and dare to soar high as we can go!

The "C" Word

*"We must embrace pain and
burn it as fuel for our journey."*
Kenji Miyazawa

I can still remember when it happened, as if it were a few minutes ago. I recall exactly where I was, what I was doing, and who I was with, because everything just stopped, my whole existence.

All I heard was the word, "Cancer." My heart stopped beating and I stopped breathing.

"Hello! Clara, are you still there?" My doctor said.

I barely whispered a *"yes."* And then the ball got rolling and nobody warned me.

"First thing you have to do is call an oncology surgeon and then go see an oncologist to see if you have to have chemo or radiation, or both, and then...."

She went on and on, and I heard everything and nothing. I wrote down the names of surgeons she recommended and then I remember her saying, *"I'm really surprised. You did everything right. You took care of yourself and you were incredibly healthy. I don't understand it. I'm really sorry. Let me know if there's anything I can do."*

A robotic *"thank you,"* came out of my mouth.

"Call me if you need anything," my doctor said.

What do I need? I thought to myself.

I looked out the window, unable to move or blink, and then it got dark.

Pause. *I had trouble writing this chapter, even after all this time. I had to write it a little bit at a time, because it brought back such trauma, intense sadness, fear, and depression. And, I must confess, I shed a few tears along with the words. I allowed myself that.*

Cancer changed me and my life without my permission. There were traces of resentment -- okay, a landslide. Unlike the movies, the cancer made my life worse. No doubt. It annihilated it on a monumental scale. I had to figure out how to put things back together, different and stronger. How the hell do I do that when I am always sick and exhausted in every way?!

After the cancer diagnosis, I didn't have a minute to think. It was cancer and that meant I was racing against time, so I got pushed into an automatic system that told me what to do, where to go, and how to feel. I had to survive first. Cut the tumor out and then everything else later. Nobody told me that the surgery, treatments, endless doctors' appointment, test after test, drawing blood, *etc.,* were the "easy" part.

I was given a small diploma with a blue ribbon wrapped around it. I graduated from radiation. *"Congratulations Clara!"* I heard technicians and nurses say, and I thanked them whole-heartedly and walked to my car like a zombie. I sat in the driver's seat, staring at the diploma, numb. I wasn't sure what it meant. I didn't know what to feel, how to respond, or even what to do. I didn't move. The numbness continued for a few more days.

The "hard" part started to unravel. The question I put on hold had to be asked. "Why me?" I don't know why I was one out of eight women to get breast cancer. I took care of myself and did all the right things, didn't smoke, rarely drank, wasn't obese, and had no history of breast cancer in the family, but still... I searched for the answers for a little while and was distraught, angry, and deeply sad. I allotted myself exact time for this. I didn't want to succumb to the quicksand of self-pity. Then, I stopped asking and got up and kept on walking.

Every cancer patient does have a choice. Get stuck asking "why" and keep waiting, or get moving; get living. It's much harder than it sounds and it's an individual journey. From time to time, I sob and feel sorry for myself, but then I snap out of it and put one foot in front of the other and just go as far as I can.

A few years later...
It was that dreaded time again. I don't know why, but they seem to come faster each time. It was time for my routine

MRI/mammogram and to see my oncologist. I should be used to this by now, but I secretly hate and fear it, all by myself.

I've become a pro. I know exactly what to do weeks in advance. Since I am always doing research, learning, and reading, and monitoring my body and symptoms religiously, I have a written list of questions and concerns for my doctor. I even read the test results, reports and look at the images.

I give myself plenty of time for my procedures and appointments. I know the best places to park and shortcuts. I know the nurses and technicians by their first names. I know what to wear. I have a set of clothes, designated just for these visits, and I am very calm and polite. In other words, I am logical and numb. I am in Mr. Spock's mode. It's how I get through it all. The few days waiting for the test results are pure hell. No words are adequate to describe it. My whole life doesn't breathe. I go through what I have to in a professional and practical manner, and survive it all. But still...I am scared. I am sad. I still cry. I will have to do this for the rest of my life. But, and that's a very big "but," I will do it and survive, one day, one test at a time, taking short and long breaths.

When I first started my cancer journey, I was frightened and passive. I surrendered all my powers and just did whatever the doctors told me to do. I was unlucky. I started off with really bad doctors who didn't listen, didn't care, and were incompetent. They hardly gave me time, rushed me in and out, and rolled their eyes when I asked about alternative and other treatment options, even though this was part of their job. I was just another routine patient to get out the door as fast as possible.

After awhile, I decided mediocre and bad care was not good enough. After all, this is cancer and it's my body and my one and only life. I had to take control of my own medical journey. So I educated myself and searched hard to create my medical team of doctors and professionals, who were competent, non-judgmental, and caring. That took awhile. But it was worth it.

I took away the most powerful lesson: *I have a choice.* It turns out we all do. No matter what stage of the illness, the final decision was mine. The buck stops with me. I wish every woman and man knew about this. But sadly, many patients end up following the standard practice of the industry, rather than their instinct, intelligence, and heart. It is still our bodies and our lives. Remember, we all have a choice.

Unfortunately, dealing with a cancer diagnosis wasn't the only difficult part. There were also often rude and careless personnel that kept me waiting half naked, incompetent technicians who nicked my nerves, made mistakes, that caused internal injuries, and health insurance companies that put money over human lives, and even friends and coworkers who judged and grew quietly distant. All this and more caused a lot of stress on top of everything. It's sad, but the truth is, even with cancer, a lot of people don't care. So, I've learned that I have to care. I have to speak up. If I don't, who will? It was a great life lesson about taking charge of my health.

What makes cancer so frightening is that it is incredibly smart, and it doesn't follow the rules, and don't make sense. I can do all the "right" things and it can still come back and kill me. So, what to do? In a nutshell, breathe, take one day at a time, do the best I can to decrease my chances of recurrence by eating healthy foods, exercising, and reducing stress and focusing on positive and happy things in life, and keep walking, one step at a time. Otherwise, it would overwhelm me and paralyze my existence.

I know everybody has something. It comes in all shapes, sizes, and forms, small or big. Buddhism states that life is suffering and the sooner we accept this, the easier and more tolerable life can be. I think this is true. There's no point in asking why questions. I leave that to the scientists who are working vigorously to find prevention and cures. In the meanwhile, cancer is about living. That is the greatest take away of it all. Just keep living, one moment, one day at a time...

Look Ma, I'm Not Stupid Any More

*"Two things are infinite:
the universe and human stupidity;
and I'm not sure about the universe."*
Albert Einstein

The other day someone asked me if I wanted to go back to my 20s, and I said politely, "ARE YOU NUTS?!!!" I got chills.

When I was younger, I had wrinkle-free smooth skin and a perky bottom, and I was able to run for miles without hyperventilating and stay up nights without getting bags under my eyes the next morning. But I was also lost, clueless, and just plain stupid. And I never want to be that way again. *Never.*

In my youth, I had no idea what I was doing, where I was going, or who the heck I was. I didn't know what I wanted to be when I grew up or anything about money or men. Now, that was scary. I don't ever want to be that vulnerable again. I didn't like being a deer in the headlights or a sitting duck. It wasn't fun. We've all learned our lessons the hard way, and now we're going to enjoy them, thank you very much. One of the best things about being middle-aged or older is we are not stupid any more. *Hallelujah!* I was worried that might never happen.

Despite what you may think of yourself and your life, you've learned quite a bit. You've learned how the world works. You may not like it, but at least you know the laws and the rules, and where things are and what to expect, most of the time. You know how to get from A to B. You know what hurts and what gives you pleasure. You know what to avoid and whom to run to. You've been around. You've learned how to survive and how to take care of yourself. Don't underestimate your life experience. It has taught you the difference from good and bad, right and wrong, and how to stand up for yourself once in a while, and where to look for your dreams, and where to get food and help when you need it. That's a lot.

When we were young and innocent, we fell for every scam and every line in the universe. At least I did. I was especially stupid when it came to men. I'd thought all men told the truth and never lied. I know. *Stupid. Stupid!* Needless to say, I learned that lesson the most painful way. I'm sure I wasn't the only one. I have the scars and nightmares to prove it.

There was purpose in our stupidity, our innocence, and our naiveté. In order to learn how people and things worked, we had to try everything ourselves, because life doesn't come with a manual, and even if it did, given human nature, we wouldn't believe it, or even read it. But we have survived thus far, and the reward is that we are not clueless and stupid any more. We may still get burned and fall on our face once in awhile, but it's not as often, and we recover faster and smarter. It's one of midlife's perks.

So the next time you're wondering if there's anything good about getting older, just remember you're not stupid any more.

I'll take not being stupid over a perky bottom any day. *No problem.*

When Dreams Die…
Something Else is Born

"You have to dream before your
dreams can come true."
A. P. J. Abdul Kalam

Did you ever have a dream?
Of course you did. I can safely say that everybody in the whole world
had a dream or two. No matter who you are, where you are, free or
not, short or tall, rich or poor, young or old, sane or insane, dreams
are universal. It's all out there, floating around in the invisible,
magical world, as we secretly hope that, with some hard work,
endless prayers, never-ending faith, a wish upon a star, a click of the
heels, and a bit of luck and magic, our dreams would come true, one
fine day.

In many ways, dreams keep us alive and keep us going, every
day. We endure all the mystery and squalor of life, walking through
dark and hopeless times often alone, because somewhere in the core
of our being we believe that someday our dreams will come true and
everything would have been worth it - the loneliness, the endless
sorrow, the injustice, the humiliation, the pain and defeat, and the
unbearable heartache. It kept us smiling despite agony and the all-
too-common human despair. We get out of bed despite aching body
parts, hunger, poverty, and horrible people who yell and degrade us,
all because we have a dream. No one and nothing could take that
away. Not even in a physical or mental prison.

But as we got older, some of our dreams started to fade and
die. Especially in midlife, we realize not all of our dreams were
destined to come true in our reality. Nobody told us that. Dreams
sometimes die like everything in life. We all had a dream that did not
come true. For reasons we'll never know, you didn't become a
ballerina, a fireman, or a dad. Your parents didn't love each other
forever, and the boy you loved gave his heart to somebody else, and
true love did not conquer all. Despite believing in the magical powers

no one could see or touch with all your heart and soul, your dreams faded away, like a runaway balloon.

When my dreams began to die, I started to wonder who decides whose dreams came true and whose did not. Who was the God of dreams? What were the rules, the rhyme, and the reason? I was willing to make sacrifices, no problem, if only the gods would tell me the rules. I was willing to obey. Foolishly, I started to ask questions, but there were no answers. There seldom are. I was angry and cried "unfair!" as I stood at my graveyard of buried dreams, weeping endlessly alone. At that moment, I learned a precious lesson about the mystery of dreams. It's okay to let them go. It's okay for a dream or two to die, because when you bury one dream, a new one is born in its place, and it might be more incredible than your old dream. Besides, dreams don't really die. They reinvent themselves beyond our own imagination and understanding.

As human beings, we can't often digest the mystery of dreams and why it works the way it does, but somehow, somebody knows what is truly best for us, and we need to believe there is a reason for everything, even if we are not allowed to understand it in this lifetime. Dreams evolve. We have to simply let go and trust the master of dreams.

I've also learned that the purpose of dreams wasn't solely to come true, but to keep us living, bringing us hope, and a bit of magic. That's the secret. Dreams keep our hearts open, and our incredible imagination unleashed beyond a restricted reality. When all else fails you, there are your dreams. And remember, there's never a short supply of new dreams to come, no matter how old you are. That's the beauty of it. Dreams are timeless. So dream on, because you never know. *You never know.*

Food & Cancer

*"Let food be thy medicine
and medicine be thy food."*
Hippocrates

Everybody was a bit different when it came to food and cancer, but we had one thing in common. Food still mattered.

When I got my cancer diagnosis, I became a soldier. I researched and learned about everything on healthy and cancer-fighting foods. I went on a strict plant-based, Buddhist-like diet to get rid of toxins and cancer cells in my body. I was so thoroughly focused, I wondered who I was.

Food was the one thing I could control right away to battle cancer and empower my body and mind. It was the only thing I had control and power over. And, I desperately needed that. Not to mention, I had other potential health issues and depression to deal with. Unfortunately, having cancer doesn't mean you won't get other diseases or another cancer.

I needed to find a food program that was healthy, easy, simple, fast, and affordable, that works now and for the rest of my life. I didn't have a lot of time, money, or energy. Unfortunately, I couldn't find anything that met my needs, so I became a self-taught nutritionist focusing on oncology nutrition and ended up creating my own food regiment for pure survival. Thus, "Food Therapy" program was born. I was more than motivated and driven to save my life and keep my sanity, once and for all. Good reasons, don't you think?

One thing that came into my mind constantly was Einstein's definition of Insanity.
"Insanity is doing something over and over again and expecting a different result." This hit me. How could I do the same thing I did in the past that might've led to cancer and expect something different, something better to occur? I had to do something new, even if it was just one thing. It was up to me. Food became my weapon and medicine, my source of infinite joy and fun.

I was always a conscientious and a relatively healthy eater. I swore off fast foods long ago and rarely drank sodas. I've also been a vegetarian for decades. But I realized that for a vegetarian, I wasn't eating a lot of vegetables or fruits. As a matter of fact, I hardly ate any and I loathed them. *What was my problem?*

When I assessed my diet, it turns out I was eating a lot of bread, pasta, and baked goods. I didn't even know it. Most people don't know what they are eating daily. Also, I loved to bake, so I made and ate cupcakes, cakes, cookies, brownies, and so forth. I also had a thing for instant ramen noodles, which was extremely bad. *Uh oh!* That had to change. So, for six months, I only ate real foods and cut out all the "white foods," like white rice, white pasta, and white bread. I also cut out dairy and caffeine. After reading that sugar could cause cancer, I happily kept my body away from all things sweet. No problem. I didn't crave it or miss it at all, because I fed my body what it needed and it was completely nurtured and satisfied. And it was goodbye instant ramen and all its cousins. I loaded up on veggies, fruits, grains, lots of water, and exercised, and managed stress. I was a soldier ant. I did it like a robot. And almost immediately, I felt better all around. My body felt light. I even lost some weight, which was not my intention, but a great bonus. *Thanks!* My stomach and gastro problems I had for decades went away, and it cured a lifetime of insomnia, along with day and night food cravings, which kept me hostage by the refrigerator. I also felt better mentally, and there were fewer visits from my depression and negative thoughts. And, everything, I mean, everything, tasted so much better, as I discovered new flavors I never knew existed from nature. And since I was the cook in my family, everybody's health improved.

I was amazed. Dumbfounded. All this, simply by eating healthy and moving my body. And I'd thought there was some exclusive secret formula or a club out there that I wasn't privy to.

Food is saving my life, and it keeps me motivated and very happy. *Happy dance!*

Honor Your Loss & Grief

*"Opportunities to find deeper powers
within ourselves come when
life seems most challenging."*
Joseph Campbell

There are many kinds of loss.
Every woman, man, child, and creatures of every kind on earth
experience it throughout their lives. It is just life. That's all the
explanation we get.

Nothing is considered more tragic than a child dying before a
parent. But that's what happened to Louise, on a cool, dark autumn
day. Louise was blessed with five children, four daughters and one
son named Jacob. He was the youngest and the most energetic of all
the kids. He was different from the start. He saw everything with
curiosity, enthusiasm, and excitement. He found people and animals,
and even the bugs, to be miracles on earth. He wanted to grow up
and become a doctor and help people in poor countries. And nothing
was going to stop him.

As he was celebrating his 32nd birthday and the birth of his
twins, Jacob suddenly collapsed onto the floor. He barely had a pulse
as the medics rushed him to the hospital with his frantic wife beside
him, confused, scared, and sobbing. Jacob had never been sick a day
in his life and now he had cancer, facing death in a few short months.
A phone call had to be made to his mom. He had to tell her that he
was going to die.

Louise stood frozen even after the call had ended. She held
onto the phone standing alone in the kitchen for an hour. She could
barely breathe or move. She couldn't even shed a tear. It just couldn't
be. Something was horribly wrong. There had to be a mistake. But
there wasn't and her son was going to die before her.

She asked all the "why" questions with fury and agony in her
red and teary eyes. But nothing changed. Nothing helped, and soon
that unimaginable day arrived. As she buried her youngest and only

son, Louise stood frozen in the snow, unable to move on. Everything, including time and life, had completely stopped for her. She wanted to die too. Nothing was alive in Louise's world any more.

Across the country in a big city, Danny had been preparing himself for an audition of a lifetime. For the past 20 years, he studied dance day and night and endured sore muscles, broken toes, excruciating back and knee pain, and hunger to keep him thin and fit. But he didn't mind. It was all part of his glorious dream. He simply wanted to dance on Broadway. That's all. So when he got a call to audition for a lead role in a musical, he practiced for weeks. Nothing was going to stop him. But on the morning of his audition, Danny got a call from the hospital. His sister overdosed and was near death. As he frantically ran to the hospital, he slipped on the icy road and landed on his back. He became paralyzed from the waist down. For almost a decade, Danny lived in anger and self-pity. Nothing mattered. And then, with the help of a caring psychotherapist, he finally let go of all the bitterness and disappointment, and decided to be alive and find another dream. Eventually, he became a dance teacher for special education students.

Adam was only six years old when his father left him, his mother, and his two sisters for a hairdresser in another state. Adam didn't understand why his father did this. But he believed it was his fault that his dad threw the entire family away. The kids started teasing him at school about not having a dad, and a few months later, Adam stopped talking.

We'll never know why losses occur. Again, we are not privileged to have an answer. So we have to deal with what we have, what we know, and what we can do. It turns out grieving has its own purpose. It helps us process our pain and sadness. Whether it's a dream, a person, a country, a pet, youth, or others, our losses matters, so, it's important to give ourselves plenty of time to grieve.

I've had my own share of losses, like most people. And in a lifetime of mourning, I've learned a few things that helped me understand the unimaginable, and cope with losses of all kinds.

First, I had to acknowledge my loss in order for the healing to begin. I recognized it and gave it the time and attention it deserved. I also allowed myself to feel and express all that surfaced from my grief. I sobbed, cried, hid, screamed, and then cried some more. I honored the experience of loss itself, cherishing the visiting memories one by one, and felt grateful to have known the person or the experience that is now physically gone. But its spirits will live on in my heart and soul, giving me courage and warmth. That will never die. Then slowly, I returned to my normal routine and continued to live and breathe. I've learned that grief is not straight forward. It evolves, sometimes going back and forth, and it's absolutely normal, and that I will be okay. I will keep going.

Mourning a loss is an individual experience and a personal journey. But where there's death, there is also birth. In moments of loss and grief, our souls are being reshaped as we develop stronger characters to endure life's sadness. After grieving, life comes back from within. The heart is stronger, becoming free from bitter heartaches and resentment that may prevent you from truly loving and living your life. Again, this is a process you should not deny yourself or your loved ones. If you deny yourself the experience of grieving, you will carry the unresolved baggage and pain and be self-destructive, which affects everything and everyone in your life. You could be in denial and be stuck, unable or unwilling to move on.

Every year, I light a candle for my losses, big and small. It's my way of saying you are still with me in my heart, but I am continuing to live. I will always remember you and be grateful you shared your beauty with me.

Loss and death is a natural part of life. It's a rite of passage to move onto the next journey. So, let them go. You still have much living and loving to do here. Your journey is unfinished.

Every time there's a loss, there's supposed to be a gain. Sometimes, we can't see it or don't even want to see it, because we are preoccupied with pain, shock, and unrelenting sadness. This happened to me when I was going through my cancer journey. There was so much loss attached to it, my head and heart were spinning. It happened during other losses, such as my youth and livelihood. And even though it felt like there was nothing to be gained by a cancer diagnosis, the gains eventually started to peek out, one by one. So, that is what I chose to spend my energy on and let go of all that had already gone. The living must live. There's still so much for us to do, so many people to love, and so many things to make right.

How to Deal with Loss

Whether it's the loss of a loved one, pets, jobs, or dreams, loss is real and it can be very painful. Here are some suggestions to help you heal and keep you moving forward.

Grieve

Allow yourself time and space to grieve and honor your loss. Your emotions are responding to the shock and pain. It's okay to feel an array of emotions like denial, anger, depression, fear, and sadness. Take the time to cry and grieve. It can be a release of deep sorrow.

Express Yourself

In a safe, trusting, and confidential environment, express your anger, fear, and sadness. Talk to a trusted individual, such as a counselor or a psychotherapist and/or do art, writing or other forms of therapy to help you express and release all your pain. Holding in your negative emotions can cause bitterness and resentment, and even get you stuck, robbing you of the present and the future.

Support Groups

Joining a support group and sharing your emotions, issues, and concerns can be an effective way to release, resolve, and connect with others who are in a similar situation. You won't feel alone.

Avoid Being Impulsive. Acting on intense emotion can have high consequences physically and psychologically. Literally, count to ten and/or remove yourself from a hostile/violent environment to assess before making any drastic decisions. You want to heal and empower, rather than become a victim in many ways.

You Still Have a Voice & Power

Some loss may leave you feeling powerless, but you have more power than you realize. But the choice is up to you. For example, as a consumer, your choices and actions can dictate the direction of politics, economy, family, and the environment. Try looking at things you can do right now to exercise those powers. Whether it's carpooling, using less gas and fuel, switching to local, organic products, or banks that invest in ethical projects, remember your choices makes a difference everyday in an effective way. There cannot be supply without a demand. You and everybody matter.

Give Yourself a Break
You are going through a lot physically and emotionally during a loss, so, give yourself a break by going on a short trip, eating your favorite food, buying yourself a small gift, or working on your favorite hobby. Reach out to a friend who is positive, caring, and funny, and hang out. Grief doesn't mean you have to be in a dark place all the time. Go outside, soak in the sunshine, go for a walk in a peaceful place. Take a nap, get a massage, relax, and breathe. You and life will go on.

Be with Caring People
Surround yourself with caring, supportive, and optimistic people who are nurturing and hopeful. Avoid negative, whining, and pessimistic people, who can bring you down and make you feel more depressed and hopeless.

Remember to give yourself plenty of time, empathy, and kindness towards yourself and others to grieve and recover. The grieving process can be both healing and empowering, if you allow it. This will eventually help you learn, grow stronger, and move forward. You still have a lot of living, giving, and loving to do. You're gonna be alright. *We all will.*

Got Problems?
Try Water off a Duck's Back

"We are all in the gutter,
but some of us are looking
at the stars."
Oscar Wilde

Each and every one of us has problems. Small or big, sane or insane, whether any of it makes sense or not, we'll have problems every single day until we die. So what do we do?

I have a friend who is 93 years old and she's never bothered by anything or anyone in life, which naturally annoyed me. So I asked if she had a secret or a formula. And this is what she said, "Live your life like water off a duck's back." Dumbfounded, I said "What?!" I had no idea what she meant and she refused to elaborate. She just told me to go find some ducks. I was on my own.

Have you ever seen water off a duck's back? Well, I haven't. So, I went to every pond and lake I could find in search of "water off a duck's back."I know it sounds a bit crazy, but sometimes you gotta actually see it with your own eyes to believe it. It took me three days of sitting hopelessly alone on park benches, surrounded by pigeons, but finally I saw it. A duck landed on the pond and splashed water on its back with its beak, and guess what? The water just slid off. It didn't stick or stay on its feathers. It just rolled off the duck's back. I got it! Nothing sticks to a duck's back. *Ohhhh.*

My friend of few words was trying to tell me not to let anything stick to my feathers. Anything bad, negative, toxic, and annoying shouldn't stick to your skin or anywhere else on you inside and out. Worrying about problems only robs you of your time, money, energy, hair, and life. It never solves anything. So just let it roll off you.

I started by having an open mind, being aware when and what problems stick to me the most and how, and then consciously I let them slide off of me mentally. With a little practice, you can control how you react to your problems and then let go of them when there's nothing much you can do about them.

Now, I know what some of you are thinking. Some problems are so big and complex you can't just let them slide off of you. And there lies the point. Where is the value in letting things get to you, where it's so monumental you no longer have control over it? It will only cloud and weigh you down, and even work against you. Give your problem the time and attention it deserves and then let it go, even for a little while. I'm happy to report that, so far, the ducks and I have shaken the water off our backs the best we can. It really helps a lot.

The smart thing is to let negative things in your life slide off of you as much as possible, and concentrate on positive things that truly matter in your life, such as family, friends, laughter, love, and eating!

Animals
Our Magical Healers

*"We should have respect for animals
because it makes better human
beings of us all."*
Jane Goodall

In the 90s, I plummeted into the darkest time of my life.
I could not find a reason to live. A long bumpy relationship ended
with bitter heartache, and my career of 15 years came to an unjust
end. On top of that, all my friends were married with kids, living in
homes of their own, and having a "normal" life. I had none of these.
And every so-called "friend" never once returned my calls. I was
headed for the abyss, completely alone, and I didn't care.

I barricaded myself in a small apartment, coming out only to
shop for food, bad food. I wore a baseball cap, baggy clothes, no
make-up, and dark sunglasses to hide the misery on my face. I didn't
want to scare anyone either. Life and people had beaten me up, and I
was tired of it all, the ridiculous charade. What was the point? It was
all over. I saw no hope.

Worried about my isolation and depression, my sister showed
up at my apartment one day, holding a small dog in her arms. He was
a rescue. He was a 6 month-old terrier mix that was going to be
euthanized because he was sick. She asked if I could help him. She
knew I had always wanted a dog, but the right time never came until
that cool April day.

Drowning in depression with barely a pulse of my own, I
reluctantly took the dog. I put him in the bathroom with every towel
and blanket I owned and some food and water, expecting him to
whine, urinate, and destroy my only bathroom the first night. But he
kept absolutely silent. He was an unusual dog from the start. He
didn't touch anything nor did he bark. As a matter of fact, he never
made a sound. For a year, I thought he was mute. The little dog was
simply sweet, happy, mellow, gentle, calm, and quiet, and he never
complained about my many flaws or quirky ways. He liked me the

way I was, even without any make-up and a few extra thighs. I named him Cosmo and we became inseparable.

I soon discovered it was impossible to stay in my apartment or have time to feel sorry for myself when I had a dog. I had to walk Cosmo, as his bladder beckoned and screamed several times a day, seven days a week, 365 days a year. I had to go and buy all the necessary dog stuff, such as dog food, leashes, collars, toys, rawhides, bowls with paw prints, flea medication, tennis balls, and stuffed animals he could tear into pieces. I had to take him to the vet for shots and to dog parks so he wouldn't get bored or become socially retarded like me.

I also couldn't avoid human beings any more. No matter how hard I tried, people started approaching, talking, and asking me questions about Cosmo. They would cross streets, stop their cars, and just come at me to talk about Cosmo, "the cutest dog they've ever seen." How rude!! Can't a woman with a dog be left alone?! They came from everywhere and petted Cosmo without my permission and asked me all kinds of dog questions. It made my depression and isolation extremely difficult. It was quite annoying. I couldn't even be a successful recluse.

Eventually Cosmo connected me with people again. Of course, I fought it every step of the way. But I started to come out of my shell, and I slowly let down my armor guard. With Cosmo by my side, life and people didn't seem so frightening any more. Rescuing and taking care of Cosmo also gave me self-worth. I had a purpose, and it felt good to feed a hungry dog and give him a warm and safe home. I made a difference in a small way. I started feeling good about myself. It was incredible. I started to wear make-up again and stopped eating everything in my refrigerator at nights.

Cosmo became my constant companion, loving me without ever complaining about my idiotic ways. He was simply an angel who saved my life quietly and willingly, without wanting anything in return, except a small treat. He was the love of my life. He brought me back to living and restored my faith in people. He rescued me, since I was the one truly sick and dying. It turns out most dogs save people's lives in many ways.

I now carry a large bag of dog and cat food in my car, and whenever I see stray animals I feed them and give them water. It's so tremendously gratifying when you feed someone hungry, four-legged or two. You should try it. Sometimes I take stray dogs home and get them adopted. Helping animals was helping myself. I've discovered that we were meant to help each other here. That's how we survive in many ways. I may give the dogs food, but the animals give me unfailing gratitude and self-worth in return. What a bargain. Hands down, I get more out of the deal.

Cosmo has also got me volunteering at animal shelters, and it has done wonders for my soul, not to mention my social life. I like people who volunteer and I like dog people. They seem to be nicer, more open, and even better looking! They are good people who care about someone other than themselves. That's rare these days anywhere in the world, and I'm lucky to know them.

Cosmo has given me so much, but there is more. He gave me something few human beings have ever given me. It is unconditional love. No matter what I do, where I am, who I am or am not, it doesn't matter. As you know, people can be so demanding, cruel, and most certainly judgmental and conditional. Cosmo just loves me 24/7/365. Cosmo's unfailing love has saved my life from withering and wasting away. No one ever did that for me.

It took a small abandoned mutt to save my life, give me hope, and unlock my chained heart. Finally, something made sense in this world and I had a reason to live: *I had to walk my dog.*

There's ton of scientific evidence now on all the positive effects animals have on humans. They literally save our lives every day in many ways. There are thousands of incredible stories of sacrifice, loyalty, and unconditional service, especially by dogs. They even help us live longer and improve our health. And, of course, they help alleviate our loneliness and to relax and enjoy life. Not too many people can do all that. At least, that's been my experience.

By the way, did you know dog people and dog walkers have more fun too? According to recent British research from Warwick University, 40 percent of dog owners stated that they make friends more easily because they have a dog. Not only that, dog people routinely initiated more social contact with other dog owners, increasing their social life. It's always easier to approach someone with a dog, rather than someone who is alone. *That's for sure.* It's amazing how much animals do for us, all that we cannot. They are truly the best healers and therapists around.

When all else fails and disappoints in a day or life, there are always, always my dogs, ready to smother me with overwhelming happiness, gratitude, wagging tails, kisses, unconditional love, and quirkiness that forces me to smile and laugh. They are truly healers and angels in disguise. I simply could not survive without them.

We humans need animals. But they don't need us. They haven't for billions of years. That puts things into perspective, don't you think? Cosmo and I help each other in an often cold and lonely world. Together we look after each other, loving with a friendship that can never be broken. Sometimes I think dogs are angels from heaven sent by God for those of us who get lost once in awhile when life becomes unbearable. Thank heaven for dogs and all the magical animals in this universe. They are the best and the truest of all healers. God bless them. God bless Cosmo. *Woof!*

A few years ago, Cosmo passed away. With him went a chunk of my heart, undying gratitude and many "thank yous and I'm sorries." I wished him well in his next journey and hope that our paths would cross again in a kinder universe. But honestly, my heart is broken and I still miss him so...

People who have never lost a pet don't realize that they cannot be replaced by another dog or a cat. They are all individuals and it takes us time to grieve and mourn our loss before we can go on. Eventually, I did.

I now have three dogs and no matter what happens in my day or life, they greet me with exuberant happiness, as if I saved their lives. They wag their tail, with their tongue hanging out, smothering me with kisses, jumps, and turns in every direction. It's really quite amazing. They never fail to make me happy. Never. And Emma, my golden, husky mix just comes and lays her head on me before my first tear drop falls. How does she know? She never leaves my side.

Few things have been constant in my life. The unfailing loyalty and unconditional love of my dogs are on the top of the list. They have always given happiness I could not find elsewhere. I could not survive or stay sane without my dogs. Thanks guys. Now, let's go for a walk!

About Your Issues

*"There's an elephant in the room.
Say hello, offer him some peanuts
and listen."*
Dr. Clara

As we go through life, we collect these annoying little things called "issues." Good or bad, everybody's got them. Some of us get them early and others get them late, but they are all there.

Issues are unavoidable, because we are human beings and we live with other human beings and that means we will eventually get hurt, ignored, disappointed, defeated, rejected, abused, humiliated, spat on, bickered with, and so on and so on. Some of us are insecure, sensitive, and emotional creatures. We have feelings, pride, ego, and other stuff that drives us nuts. So what do we do about these issues?

The first thing to do is acknowledge them. You can't pretend not to have them. Denial is a harmful thing. The longer you deny, the harder it will become. And don't kid yourself; issues don't just sit inside of you taking a long nap. They spread like a disease, affecting every aspect of your life and relationships whether you know it or not, or whether you choose to know it or not.

Most likely you know what your real issues are, but because they're difficult and painful to face, you've pushed them into the unconscious, or you've tricked your mind to believe you don't have any, or you've buried them in the backyard in the middle of the night when no one was looking. We're very good at that. People in major denial bury it under a lot of things like work, alcohol, drugs, and food, including a ton of chocolate, or in someone else's backyard.

The cold hard fact is you have to face your issues. It's the only way to be free from them. And it's not as scary as you might think. I know. I've faced most of mine, if not all. And the good news is that you don't have to face them alone. There are now more resources than ever to help you. Seek help from a counselor, a friend, a pastor, support groups, a monk, or a psychotherapist. It will lead to peace of mind, and everything and anything is worth that.

By the way, issues are not for nothing. They have great value. They give you insight into who you really are and what's really bugging you. They show you your weaknesses and strengths, and take you into both the light and dark sides of you. It's actually quite fascinating and enlightening, if you allow them.

It's time. You've run out of excuses and you're old enough to do it. So acknowledge your issues, remembering everyone has them and you're not alone, and it's nothing to be ashamed of. The only shameful thing is avoiding them. It takes courage to look at your issues, and you have it. I admire anyone willing to do it. So go for it, and don't let issues dictate your life any more.

Nature
Everybody's Sanctuary

"Nature is not a place to visit.
It is home."
Gary Snyder

Emily Dickinson, the famous poet and recluse who spent most of her life in her father's house alone, found beauty, life, and solace in nature. There, she observed the seasons and saw the natural order of life in growth, decay, and rebirth. Trees, flowers, leaves, snow, soft flowing breezes and amazing animals outside her window gave her endless fascination, comfort, and unconditional love, that she could not find among the human world. People were often the culprit of her pain and loneliness, but in nature, she found a world of kindness and gentleness. She wasn't alone there. "I created and lived in my sovereign woods." I think a lot of people can relate.

The first place I ran to in times of heartache was nature. There in the arms of majestic trees, blue skies, and crystal waters, I took refuge from a harsh and discriminating human world. In nature, there was no time, no responsibility, no titles, nor obligations, and no humans! I was not judged or labeled by looks, age, color, gender, money, or weight. I was one of its creatures and that was all. I was no better or worse. I was free to do nothing, be nothing, stay still, and breathe. I was part of Earth, no questions. There was just pure harmony and acceptance. There were no man-imposed rules. I was free to be me. It was pure beauty that was larger than I. It was perfection. All that humans were not.

In nature, I also felt ageless and timeless. I felt I belonged. I was part of something larger than the human design. Nature also gave me a sense of adventure and serenity. I discovered a sense of calmness and inner peace I could not find in mankind. Through sun, wind, air, and water, I found my soul blowing in the wind. I rested, healed, and came back to life.

In the gentle nest of nature, I grieved for the passing of my youth and released my fears of old age. I gained strength from the womb of Mother Earth. It put all things into perspective as confusion melted away. I had come home after a long and grueling journey with many scars and wounds. Nature gave me physical, emotional, and spiritual oxygen. I was finally able to unload all my burdens and rest.

I often immerse myself in the comfort of flowers, the hummingbirds, and the deep blue ocean and find a deep, spiritual happiness. It's no wonder most of us retreat to the mountains or the ocean, to relax and rejuvenate during vacations. Perhaps this is why gardening is so popular and therapeutic. It's a great feeling to touch earth, cultivate, and watch its incredible circle of life unfold, as it also provides us with food and nourishment for our mind and soul.

Go back to nature as much as you can. Find comfort there and connect. It's your true home. Be part of it. We are made from soil, plants, air, and wind. When you get to know the true beauty of nature and its creatures, you will get to know yourself. It will also alleviate your pain and put your life and yourself into a larger perspective.

Tragically, our planet, our only home is in danger. We are destroying our sanctuary, our place of healing, joy, and spirituality. And there's only one culprit, MAN.

We cannot replace nature or earth. So while you are healing in the woods, basking in the sun, or riding the blue waves of the ocean, do your part in protecting and respecting our one and only home. Don't pollute. Pick up after yourselves. Respect wildlife and admire them from a distance. Don't impose your selfishness. And plant as many trees, plants, flowers, and food whenever possible.

Remember, if Earth dies, we die. So let's save it and save ourselves.

Connect With "Real" People.
I Swear, They're Out There

"Friend, Good. Alone, Bad."
Frankenstein

The water company had no choice but to send someone out to the property. They suspected busted water pipes, which were tripling the water bill and draining the water supply. It sent numerous notices to the homeowner, but there was no response.

When the water official arrived at the property, he got more than he could ever imagine. Inside the house was a man sitting on a couch in front of the TV, which was still on. His automatic payment to his electricity company from his bank account took care of that. The man had been dead for months and no one, absolutely no one, knew about it.

The unknown man died alone in front of the TV. No one came by. No one left messages on his answering machine. No one was worried that he hadn't been seen or heard from. He was absolutely alone. If it weren't for the water pipes that burst, he wouldn't have been discovered for even a longer period. What a way to go. What a way to die. He lived everybody's worst nightmare. He died alone.

One of the hardest lessons I learned in life was if I didn't want to get old by myself and die alone, I had to work on connecting with people. It was up to me, not fate, parents, or Santa. And it had to start now.

It's funny how people who fear being alone will consciously or unconsciously sabotage relationships, friendships, and marriages, so they will end up being absolutely alone. Well, STOP THAT!! Find out why you are doing this and stop it, before you truly end up alone.

There's no doubt that it's tougher to connect with people now more than ever. There are more of us (more than 7 billion) and yet we couldn't be further apart. Thanks to technology and modernization, we can survive without ever talking or seeing someone's actual face. That's frightening.

I've been working with a colleague for the past 11 years, and in all that time, I have never heard her voice or seen her face. All work was done by email, fax, and overnight express. Isn't that sad? Tragic really, and yet this is all too common. We live in a time where it's normal to never speak to or see our own neighbors. We are missing the whole point of being on this planet together. We need each other like food and water to survive, physically, emotionally, and spiritually, and yet we can't even look at each other in the elevator.

If you don't want to be alone, the answer is simple. Go and be with real people. Take the time, swallow your pride, reach out, open up your heart, your mind, and your world. You gotta make the effort. Join groups, clubs that interest you, professional and alumni associations, and so forth. Search high and low for good, real people. It may take a little longer to find them, because real folks don't draw attention to themselves, and they are rarely in the spotlight, but they are out there being extraordinary in an ordinary life. And don't forget to be a real, genuine person yourself. Fakes, flakes, and shallow individuals don't get very far.

Work on connecting with people every day, and make sure they are people who are genuine and caring and REAL. No phonies allowed any more. We've had enough of them in our lives.

Remember, whatever you do, don't ever sign up for automatic payment to the electricity company and sit alone watching TV. Never ever! Instead, go out and meet some folks. Smile. Give them a firm handshake, and say, "Have you heard about the guy who died alone in front of his TV..."

Self-Esteem
Your Greatest Weapon, Ally & Best Friend

*"You yourself, as much as anybody
in the entire universe, deserve your
love & affection."*
Buddha

What do you think is the difference between someone who succeeds and someone who fails?

Have you watched TV and wondered why an untalented and unattractive actor or an anchorperson made it so far in their careers? Have you wondered why your co-worker, who is missing half a brain is always getting the promotions? Have you watched an Olympic competition with two equally skilled athletes to see one always succumb to pressure? It's not about being smart or having talent. That comes later. It's about something you cannot see, but it's powerful enough to create magic and make dreams come true.

It's called self-esteem. It's about believing in yourself no matter what. Without it, you will always question yourself in life. Have you seen someone with a lot of self-esteem? I have, and it's mesmerizing. It draws me to them. They are confident and self-assured, and they are certain they will succeed because they rely on the single greatest source in their lives: Themselves.

Even on the playground at school, you can see it happening. The bullies don't pick on kids who are confident and unafraid. It's always the ones who are not sure of themselves, the ones who lack self-esteem.

Some people are born with a lot of self-esteem, while others are given encouragement early in life, which naturally increases their self-esteem. Sadly, some of us lose it because someone criticized us, put us down, and belittled us as being inferior, unworthy, and stupid when we were young. I was one of them. My parents have always encouraged me from the day I was born, but when we immigrated to America, my American teachers told me repeatedly that I was an inferior human being because I was not White, and I would end up being nothing better than a "maid." I was just a kid, a scared little kid thrown into a foreign country with foreign people, speaking a foreign language. I had no reason to believe they weren't telling me the truth. I believed them. So the damage began. And from then on, I believed I was second class in America, and I didn't deserve anything other than being a maid. It affected every aspect of my life, including my career and my relationships with people, including men.

Once we lose our self-esteem, we have to work very hard to get it back. But it's worth the effort because it is something we must have in order to stand on our own two feet in life. In order to gain your self-esteem, you need to start focusing on positive things in you and your life. You also need to reduce or eliminate negative things in your life that make you feel like you're worthless. Sometimes that could be a person. Don't let them anymore. We are old enough to stand up to them now. Stay away from negative and toxic people as much as you can.

Try focusing on one thing in your life that makes you feel worthy, strong, and proud, and then build from there. It's like planting a seed, watering and nurturing it every day, so that someday it will become a strong and majestic tree. Surround yourself with supportive people and allow them to nourish you. You may not think you deserve it, but you do. Go into therapy to resolve repressed issues and strengthen your mental power.

Work on developing your self-esteem consciously every day. It matters throughout your whole life. If you don't have yourself, who does? And what sweet revenge it would be to all those people who picked on you.

Bullies are still around. So work on developing an unshakeable self-esteem. It will be your greatest weapon, ally, and best friend throughout your whole life.

Find Your Community
Find Your People

"A community is a must for our happiness."
Unknown

Jethro was the first in line.

He weathered two days of freezing temperature, rain and snow, people trying to cut in, and his parents' wrath, all to see the latest saga of "Star Wars." When a reporter asked, if it was about the costume, the story, science fiction, or Chewbacca, he replied, "Nope. Those things are fun, but it's really about being in a community, where we share a passion. I've met the most amazing, coolest people who have become my closest friends." Jethro knows a thing or two about this. He was bullied most of his young life and never had a single friend to call his own, until now.

At one time in my life, I didn't have a single community. I wasn't married. I didn't have a job, kids, money, boyfriend, or any hobbies. I know. Sad. And these were the most common ways people found communities, so I was thoroughly out of luck.

My married friends had their married couples' community. The ones with the kids had the school community and the parenting community. Even the divorced folks had a community of their own; so did the single moms and dads. They had clubs, meetings, outings, websites, parties, support groups, and blogs. The seniors had it the best. They actually had community centers with every recreation under the sun, including free disco lessons, tapas extravaganzas, art festivals, and bingo every Tuesday night, just to mention a few. They also got senior discounts almost everywhere in everything. They traveled and ate well. They were having so much fun that I asked if I could join their community, but they said I was too young. *Shoot!* I told them I looked younger than my age, but they didn't buy it. I begged and even offered to teach them the cha cha, but they all said, "Sorry kid, come back in a few years." You bet I will.

Why do we need a community?

A community gives us a sense of belonging and acceptance, security and balance, and freedom. It's a place to relax and just be you. It's where like-minded people can share similar values and beliefs.

People in solid communities tend to be more productive and are generally healthier and happier. We are welcomed and supported with open arms, and we can explore our possibilities and dreams and express our voices and power, together without judgment or discrimination. It's a place where we can get a hug for no reason, a pat on the back, or a shoulder to lean on. It's where we can get a cup of coffee with a dose of empathy and understanding. What a magical place.

So how do you find a community? First, you have to ask yourself a few questions and visualize your community. What does it look like and who are "your people"? What do they look like? What are they doing? What are their values, causes, interests, and goals? Do you want your community to fight for a cause, raise money for a playground, share an undying passion or hobby, go rumba dancing every Saturday night, or all of the above? What do you want your community to be about, and what is your role in it? It helps to write it down as well.

If you can't find a community, start one yourself. That's what I did. I could not find a community I could fit into and be comfortable in, so I went ahead and started it myself, and it was easy. For example, in the Midwest, a bunch of Americans started a Korean drama fan club. These were folks who accidentally stumbled onto Korean-language programming on TV and started watching Korean soap operas with English subtitles. So guess what? They started a community where fans of Korean dramas got together and talked about their favorite shows, actors, scenes, and lines, while eating Korean food with kimchi, and having loads of fun. The best part was they were making new friends and sharing a common interest, a passion that connected them. That's what it's about.

By the way, you can have as many communities as you want. It's completely up to you. For example, my friend Jack has a community of folks who are obsessed with food and healthy eating. They get together once a month just to cook, eat, laugh, and then eat some more. He loves it. He also has a community where they dance like mad. They go tango, cha cha, rumba, and salsa dancing. Nothing can hold them back. It's not about being good or bad, but just boogieing and having a good time together. My neighbor Betty has her wonderful animal community, where she rescues and helps hungry, abused, and homeless dogs, cats, rabbits, and even an alligator, with other folks who are also compassionate towards animals. They often have bake sales, car wash, and parties to raise money. They also open up their homes to foster frightened and unloved dogs and cats, and give them a warm and safe place to heal and come back to life.

In a community, we support each other in our commonalities and make a difference on all levels. We do it all together. We are not alone in our endeavors. A community is where we can find understanding, support, connection, love, fun, and lots of jokes, while being who we really are. It is the base for a healthier body and mind and of course, happiness. *Yes!*

Did you know the need to belong to a community and its rituals have been around since ancient times? It has been built into our psyche over thousands of generations. It's that crucial. It's a survival tactic, too. We survive better in packs, like in the animal kingdom. There's definitely strength in numbers. It's been proven that when we are alienated, we are more susceptible to medical and psychological illnesses and premature death. We sure don't want that.

One of the worst things for us is isolation. It can cause all kinds of maladies to the body, mind, and spirit, so seek out and find a community and make sure that your community consists mainly of positive, good, and happy people.

Woman in the Underworld

"I have a secret sorrow.
Can you guess what it is?
It is inside of me and it never dies."
Dr. Clara

I was lying half naked on a gurney in the hallway of the emergency room. All I could do was stare at the brown rain spots on the ceiling. I couldn't move. I had asked for a blanket over an hour ago, but it was a Saturday night and gunshot and stab wounds were more of a priority than someone with an unexplainable and excruciating pain in the brain.

It took me hours just to get into the emergency room after waiting with the other unfortunate saps who got sick on a weekend. I was lying in a cold, smelly hospital like a corpse pushed to the side. I could hear people rustling and passing by me like in Grand Central Station, but no one noticed that I was alive and in a great deal of pain. I endured the pounding migraine. It felt like my head was being kicked by 10 heavyweights all at once, over and over, and it was beginning to split open. I bit my lower lip, while tears rolled down the side of my face and past my ears. I gripped the sheets with my fingers and tightened every muscle of my body with the last ounce of life left in me. I'd never known such unrelenting pain and I'd had it more than 48 hours. I cried and cried silently, praying and begging, but still no one came. I was freezing. The pain got worse. This was the first time I had ever been in an emergency room in my life. It would not be my last. I screamed.

Three months earlier, my therapist threatened to call the police. He got scared. He's heard me talk about death before, but this time he felt he had to do something. Then I got scared. I told him not to call the police. I wasn't suicidal. I lied. Then he insisted that I go see a psychiatrist he trusted. So I did.

Walking toward the office of my very first psychiatrist, I felt ashamed that my life had come to this. With each step I took, I felt I was losing myself; being disconnected. I didn't know my life or myself any more. I felt mechanical, numb, and overwhelmingly defeated. I hated myself. I was convinced that it was because I was stupid, weak, hopeless, and all other things shameful that I found myself walking towards a psychiatrist's office to be drugged. It meant I could not solve my own problems. I've rarely taken drugs even from a drug store, and now I was going to take a brain-altering medication so I would not be depressed or have any more thoughts of killing myself. I blamed myself over and over. There was no history of depression in my family. So why am I the only one having this sickness I can neither see nor touch? What is wrong with me?! What did I do that was so bad?! I was silently hysterical.

I was out of the psychiatrist's office in less than 25 minutes with a slip of paper. After asking me three questions, she took a prescription pad and wrote something only she and a handful of pharmacists could decipher. It was a popular antidepressant. They've become as common as vitamins, but still I could not believe this was happening to me. The doctor didn't give me any warnings or instructions. She told me to take it every day and if it didn't work after a few weeks, stop taking it. She would give me another drug. End of session.

Everything seemed surreal. I felt like I was in a foreign movie with abstract scenes I couldn't grasp. Like a zombie, I went to the drug store, still carrying the shame and blame for being "sick." Barely lifting my head, I got my meds and went home and cried alone.

Two weeks went by and I wasn't feeling any different. I had called my psychiatrist but she was on vacation. So, as she told me, I stopped taking the medication and that's when I got into trouble. The next morning, I woke up with an agonizing pain in my head. At first I'd thought it was a bad migraine. After a while, the pain was so bad, I couldn't stand or walk. I barely reached the phone and called my poor parents and they carried me into the emergency room. By this time, I was in so much pain, I was sobbing, as I was hurting all over with no control over my body.

It had now been more than three hours, lying on a gurney in a cold hospital hallway, freezing from not having a blanket or a jacket on me. My poor parents were frantic and worried to death, waiting outside the whole night in their pajamas. I didn't think it was possible but the pain got worse and I couldn't endure it anymore, and out of nowhere, I screamed from the top of my lungs for what seemed like an eternity. I was dying and it hurt so much I had to scream over and over, and that's when a doctor finally came over and examined me. I didn't even know I screamed.

He couldn't figure out what was wrong with me. After all the waiting, he told me I had to ride it out and there was nothing he could give me for the pain. He put me on an IV but it was of little help. So for the next 72 hours, I laid in my parent's bed screaming with a brutal pain in my head. At times it hurt so bad I banged my head against the wall and hurled my body onto the ground. It was the longest three days of my life. I will never forget it. Needless to say, I was traumatized. I never wanted to feel that kind of pain again. But I did.

I discovered later that one should not stop taking antidepressant altogether. You need to taper off slowly, a little bit at a time; otherwise what happened to me would happen. The psychiatrist should have warned me. She never returned any of my numerous and desperate phone calls, pleading for help.

Ten years went by and my depression persisted. Reluctantly, I tried the antidepressants again, as an insistence from my therapist. It landed me in the ER again, not only with the excruciating pain in the brain, but uncontrollable seizures throughout my whole body, that made me fall and hit my head on a sharp object and pass out.

This was it. It was finally clear to me that medication wasn't going to help me with my depression, so I vowed to search for an alternative, safe, and long-term method that would help me for life. I went on a quest, searching everywhere for natural ways to help me manage my depression, so I don't think about killing myself every single day, and I can have my life and dreams back once and for all.

It was a long, painful, lonely, and arduous journey, but it worked. After many years, I finally discovered my set of "healing methods," which helps me deal with depression on a daily basis. They are natural, drug free, affordable, non invasive to the body, effective and long term.

There is no cure for depression or for any mental illness yet. So, I depend on myself to manage my symptoms-- to be in control over the depression and not the other way around, so I can function and not have my life be robbed by a mental illness. It has done decades of that.

In my hellish depression journey, I discovered an unlikely gift inside of me, as I reached a dark and deep part of my being, I would never have known otherwise. It may sound weird, but I am grateful for that. My perspective in life is more intense, deeper, sensitive, and meaningful, and I can empathize more with others in their suffering.

I've also made peace with my depression. I don't see it as the monster I feared and loathed for so long. After all, it is a part of me and it seems to be there with some reason and purpose. Seeing it this way -- changing my perspective -- has alleviated my symptoms greatly. I am not a victim any more. In fact, I've had many conversations with my depression, as I asked questions like, *"Why are you here, why did you choose me, what do you want, what can I do to help you leave?"* I was amazed at the answers that came out of my own self.

When people ask me to describe depression and how it feels, I often refer to the dementors in Harry Potter. Do you remember? They thrive in filth, decay, and despair. A long, dark, skeletal, boney figure creepily reaches for your soul and then it sucks out all that is good, positive, and happy in you, including all your hope, energy, spirit, and life, and leaves you soulless with only dark and miserable memories. *Yup!* That's depression. It's worse than these words can describe or in the movie, because it lasts for so long, and you feel alone and there are no magic wands to get rid of them. And sadly, you cannot feel the love around you at all. It truly is a horrible and cruel disorder to say the least. If you want to destroy someone's body, mind, and soul, depression would be the way to do it.

My depression now rarely causes havoc in my life, but when it tries, I know what to do. I am in control. I have resources and the power of reaction. Like Persephone, I am no longer a prisoner of the Underworld, but a guide for unfortunate souls who fall into the mental dungeon. If we are gonna go to hell and back, we might as well come out with something brilliant. And I did. Thank goodness. So, have hope everyone.

Persephone

In Greek mythology, Persephone was abducted by Hades, the God of the Underworld, where dying souls withered away in deep, dark state of death and hopelessness. When Demeter, Persephone's mother tried to free her, Hades tricked Persephone and eventually, she was forced to spend half of the year in the Underworld, serving as a guide to the frightened souls, and the other half in the upper world with her mother. For me, the Underworld often symbolized depression.

Hello Mental Health

"The best way out is always through."
Robert Frost

I often think mental disorders are one of the cruelest facts of life. It's hard to imagine or understand unless you've seen or experienced it yourself. I've done both for decades now. It was hell in my own body and mind. It was the coldest, darkest, and the loneliest place in one's existence. I was dead alive, if you can imagine that. I wish it on no one.

Did you know that 450 million people on the planet are affected by mental and behavioral problems at any given time? Depression alone affects more than 100 million people a year. It's the number one disability in the world. IN THE WORLD! Sadly, it affects people of all ages and races. In the U.S., more than 20 million people suffer from depression and more than 90 percent of suicides are attributed to mental health disorders.

According to the World Health Organization, more than 1 million people worldwide kill themselves each year. By the year 2020, it is estimated that 1.53 million people will die by suicide. That's one death every 20 seconds. In the past 50 years, suicide rates have increased by 60 percent worldwide, and it's getting worse. That's equal to the number of deaths from war, aids, and homicide put together. Just imagine people taking their own lives because the pain is so great and they see absolutely no hope. Do you know what that feels like? It's something you cannot fathom unless you've been there.

Mental illness is complicated further by civilization and modernization, where we are ironically becoming more isolated and compartmentalized in a world of more than 7 billion people. As we grow further away from nature and each other, and who we truly are, we are becoming more depressed and more alone, which causes us to retreat into our heads, where reality could be distorted. All this can lead to many illnesses of the mind, not to mention broken hearts and lives.

Mental illness is absolutely real!

There's still a shame factor attached to mental health in many cultures and societies, because it cannot be seen, and thus, we fear it. A lot of people cannot understand why some people are paranoid, can't come out of their homes, hear voices no one else can hear, or are obsessed with germs, or can't get out of bed, or display "abnormal" behavior that are different from everybody else. Unless you've been there, it's hard to comprehend. But let me ask you, if you want to understand someone "different," what would you do? Most people will impose their perspective and values onto them without knowing it. That's why we think anyone who doesn't behave like us is "abnormal." But that's a subjective term. Who's to say what is normal and what is abnormal?

When I started my pre-doctoral internship, a group of psychotherapists decided to have some fun at the expense of an inexperienced, eager, yet frightened intern. They decided to give me all the cases that no one wanted: the hard ones; the impossible ones; the dangerous ones. *Thanks!* But to their dismay, these cases turned out to be the best experience in my internship, and some of them even became study cases for future interns.

One of the groups no one wanted to run was a schizophrenia support group for men. They were deemed "difficult" and "hopeless." My supervisor told me to just make sure they were on their medication. That's it.

When I walked into my first schizophrenia support group session, the men sat lifeless, looking lethargic, and barely moving in complete silence. Most of them were on medication and they looked like zombies. They ignored me. They were mentally ill, not stupid. They knew no one wanted to be with them. The former psychotherapist did the bare minimum, underestimated them, and cut the sessions short. I introduced myself and eagerly and genuinely took an interest in their stories. The approach I used was that what they said, what they saw, what they found to be the "truth" in their lives, was absolutely real and it exists. Think about it. What is real or true? Isn't that up to the individual? If they said they've heard voices and seen people that no one else can see, I believed them. Just because I could not see them didn't mean they did not exist. I asked them to tell me more about the voices, people, and demons. After all, they were part of these patients, so I wanted to understand all of it without judgment and with complete trust. They were here because they were different from most people and they could not function in our "normal" society. This didn't make them less of a human being. On the contrary, they were more real and truthful than the "normal" people in the office.

Mental health disorders are prevalent worldwide and they are just as real as any physiological diseases. They can cause a lot of pain and they can kill. So don't ignore the symptoms or signs of mental problems. They are nothing to be ashamed of. It's only shameful if you don't acknowledge them.

Don't deny yourself the right to be treated. You don't need to suffer needlessly or alone. There are numerous treatments available, including conventional, complementary, and alternative methods. Educate yourself, be aware of your emotions, keep an open mind, and monitor your own symptoms. Writing them down always helped me. Check your family history of mental illnesses, and ask for help. Remember, you are not alone. *Ever.*

Friendship
It's What Matters from Beginning to End

"You cannot be a failure
if you have friends."
Unknown

Do you know the story of Owen and Mzee (mm-ZAY)? They are the coolest friends in the world.

When a tsunami hit in 2004, it left baby Owen stranded on a reef. Rescuers worked for hours to save the little orphan from the sea's salt waters. When he was finally brought to a sanctuary, he was understandably petrified. So as soon as the truck door opened, he dashed out and hid behind the nearest resident, Mzee, who was resting and minding his own business under a tree. Owen felt much better.

Mzee, which means "wise old man" in Swahili, had been a loner for decades. He kept to himself and no one bothered him. He liked it that way. That is until a 600-pound baby hippo attached himself to Mzee, who was only a 130-year-old tortoise. He tried to crawl away from Owen at his record speed, but the hippo had no trouble following the tortoise around. The whole day and night, Owen stayed right next to Mzee, and by the next morning, the hippo and tortoise were found snuggling, and before long, they became inseparable. Soon the two of them were eating together, sleeping together, swimming together, and definitely rubbing noses together. They looked out for each other. They were not alone any more in the scary human world.

Not a single scientist or wildlife expert could explain their friendship. A mammal and a reptile have never been friends. But Owen and Mzee, who had lost their mothers, herds, and homes, found life, hope, and friendship in each other. All that mattered now was they were friends for life.

I love the story of Owen and Mzee. They inspire me and so many others. Their story reminds us how precious friendship can be and that it can be found in the most unexpected situations. And above all, it doesn't matter what you are, how old you are, or how much you weigh (600 pounds!). You can have friends, too. That's the beauty of it all. Friendship can happen anywhere and with anyone, even a hippo and a tortoise. So there's hope for all of us.

Remember when we were kids? Friends were the most important things in our lives. We walked to school together, played together, hung out together, sang together, danced together, went to slumber parties together, giggled together, ate together, talked about "Jimmy, the coolest guy in school," together, annoyed our parents together, and shared our dreams together. We simply did everything together. That was our happiness.

Then somewhere on the way to becoming a grown-up, our friends got lost in the shuffle of life. Careers, men, kids, bills, PTAs, office politics, titles, status, money, in-laws, looking good, and being with the "right people," took over our lives. In the grown-up world, friends became people who could help you with your careers, do you favors, and help you get ahead in work and society. We forgot about our real friends.

Then our kids left for college; gray hair started protruding; boyfriends, girlfriends, and spouses came and went; fair-weather friends turned out to be fakes; and our titles and money didn't seem to be the most important thing in the world. As we approached the mercy of midlife, we wondered where our childhood friends went: the pals who loved us for no reason at all and the ones we played with until it turned dark outside, while our parents screamed at us to come inside. We were missing a true connection in life. We found ourselves alone in a cool and breezy autumn midlife.

Friends seem harder to come by these days, especially as we get older. For some reason, friends were easier to find back in school. Perhaps we were pure and innocent back then, and not so jaded by life. The truth is we need friends throughout our lives. Sometimes we forget about our friends in the hectic routine of our days. We pencil in our lunches. But now, more than ever, we need to connect with friends again, because it matters in our survival.

According to a study from researchers at the University of Oxford, the more friends you have, the higher your tolerance for pain will be. More Friends = Less Pain. There are many similar studies that prove friendship and human connection contribute to meaning, longevity, joy and happiness.

Real friends don't judge you by age, wrinkles, income, titles, marital status, height, and weight. And they will understand and comfort you through all of life's insanity, mystery, and surprises, good and bad. Friendship is the key to getting through life with meaning, support, love, and laughter. Life is never quite as bad, lonely, or sad when we have friends. They are always there. So make the effort to make new friends and rebuild old friendships, and don't forget to be a great friend yourself. When you have true friends, you will never be alone. Imagine that.

So have a slumber party. It's time once again to laugh together, giggle together, annoy our kids, wives, in-laws, relatives, and husbands together, eat and drink together, talk about "Jimmy, still the coolest guy!" and share our dreams together, *forever.*

Parents
Make Peace Before It's Too Late

*"I don't think my parents liked me.
They put a live teddy bear in my crib."*
Woody Allen

Most of us see our parents as strong and smart people who never have sex and will live forever. But by the time we are in midlife, we realize that our parents have grown older too. They are now senior citizens. When did this happen?

The roles get reversed. Our parents need us now. We have become the caretakers to mom and dad who raised us and gave us life. And, despite all the news reports that seniors are living healthier and longer, many are plagued with illness, neglect, abuse, depression, and isolation. Americans have never been known to respect and care for its senior population. Shame on us.

Let's face it. We are all selfish to some degree. We don't take the time to think about our parents, what they are doing, how they are getting along or how they are feeling. We are too wrapped up in our own lives, and we believe our parents will always be there for us and live forever. But they won't.

It's painful for many of us to see our parents getting older, weaker, and sicker. The same people who were able to work all day and solve every problem in the world for us now walk with canes, go to the doctor's weekly, depend on medications, need assistance standing up and sitting down, and make those old people's grumpy noises. You see and feel your parent's mortality. It's there and it's frightening.

I can't imagine my world without my mom and dad. I can't bear to think about it. We are close, although we bicker from time to time, but when things get tough, my parents are the first and last ones there always, making sacrifices without complaints.

It's one of those life truths that we have to swallow and deal with. Our parents will most likely die before us. And since time is not on our side, we need to make peace with our parents now. Whether you have a good relationship with your folks or a bad one, or none at all, make the attempt to spend more time with them. You don't even have to talk. You just need to be with them. This is for your peace of mind more than anything. Each day counts. Nobody knows when our time is up.

I interviewed dozens of people who have lost their parents and sought their advice, and they all said the same thing: Make peace with your parents. Be good to them while they are alive, so you won't have any regrets or guilt. And simply say what you've been holding back all these years: Thank you. I'm sorry. And I love you. Do it while they're still here. There's nothing you can do once they are gone. So make peace for both of your hearts and souls.

If your parents passed away before you could make peace, do it posthumously. In a quiet space, light a candle, place a picture of your parent(s), or their name(s), or an object that connects you to them, and then simply say all that is in your heart — all that you held back because of misunderstanding, bitterness, hatred, immaturity, or fear. And send them off to a peaceful place, as you start the grieving and mourning process that will set you free from a burdened heart.

There's no right or wrong here. Give yourself and your parents a voice, and then set everyone free.

When I Grow Up, I Want To Do Something I Love

*"I'd rather be a failure at something I enjoy
than be a success at something I hate."*
George Burns

A few years ago, I watched a TV program that interviewed women and men who achieved inner peace. The question was how they did it, when so few of us could. One of the people interviewed was an elderly Native-American woman, who retired from working at the post office for 40 years and then simply started basket weaving. She just started basket weaving in the back of her house for no reason at all. She loved it. It had nothing to do with money, responsibility, or time, and no one had to know about it, approve of it, or think anything of it. She just loved basket weaving. It was her thing.

Before she knew it, she made a lot of baskets, and her neighbors came by and asked to buy them because they were so beautiful, not to mention authentic and homemade. At first, she gave them away until her daughter told her to sell them, and so she did. The Indian woman didn't need the money. She was happy living in a modest house that had belonged to her family for generations, and her retirement fund was sufficient to cover her basic needs. She didn't need or want more. So she donated the money to feeding the homeless people and animals in her community.

It was just basket weaving in her spare time after retirement in the back of her house, but it was magic to those who felt her gift of love. It gave hungry people and animals food to eat. It gave them dignity. It gave them hope and life. And all this gave the basket weaver inner peace.

Let me ask you. What do you want to be when you grow up... again? How about doing something you love? *Far out!* It sounds so simple, and yet so few of us actually do it. When we were kids, it was natural to do something we loved. There was no other way. But somewhere on that gray journey of becoming a grown-up, we turned into little robots, getting up at the same time, going to the same place, wearing the same clothes, doing the same thing, where we did what was "responsible, acceptable, proper, and practical."

In some of my jobs, I was fortunate enough to have a tiny window in my office. I would stare out for hours, months, years, basically wanting to jump out of it because I hated my jobs. I had no idea how I got there. Sometimes, I'd thought I was in a nightmare or in a bad sitcom. But nope, it was reality. I loathed my job. Once, I wanted to bang my head against the wall but my boss would not allow it. He said I would have to pay for the damage. That's all he cared about. I had to be insane to go to a job I hated day in and day out, right? Sadly, I wasn't alone. More than half of Americans spend a third of their lives in a job they hate. I wonder if they look out of windows, too.

Nothing depletes our spirit and energy more than being involved in a job that we detest. Have you seen someone who hates his/her job? All life has drained out of them. There's no one home any more. They are no longer alive.

We know this much: We have just this one life to live, so why waste it on a job that we can't stand? Yes, we have "responsibilities" and "mouths to feed," but if the work is hurting you, it will hurt everyone around you, too, and unknowingly, your kids will adopt your behavior and belief that it's okay to waste away in a miserable state for money. Unless somebody breaks this cycle, it can trickle down for generations. Don't we want to pass on something positive, so their lives could be happier, or at least have a chance at it?

I used to wonder about rock stars. How did they get to be so lucky? They got to make music, sing, dance, and make an amazing living, while being adored by fans, traveling around the world, and marrying international supermodels. What's up with that?!

I used to secretly pretend to be a rock star in my bedroom, jumping around, over and under the bed, holding a spatula as a mike, and scaring my poor dog to death. Let's face it. We all wanted to be a rock star. It was our fantasy. But only a few of us end up living our dreams.

At midlife, I can no longer be a rock star, a ballerina, and a few other things, and I can't quit my day job yet. But I've discovered that I can still do what I love without giving up my whole life or starving to death. It doesn't have to be all or nothing.

Do something you love part time, on the side, as a hobby, or whenever you can squeeze it in. The point is to do it somewhere in your life for your sanity, for your spirit, and for those you love. This is food for your soul. It doesn't always have to be in the form of a job or a career, and it doesn't necessarily have to bring in money. That will follow. Whether it's once a week, once a month, once a year, the point is to simply do what you love. You can do it alone or with a friend, anywhere, any time.

Keep it simple and real.
Maybe you won't make it to Carnegie Hall, but you can make it to the community theatre, or sing as a volunteer at a nearby children's hospital, or become a basketball coach, while waiting for your big break. You can clear out the garage one weekend and build that "dream rocking chair," or set aside an hour a week to start that novel you've been talking about forever. Give up one hour of TV a day and you can probably knit sweaters for your whole family. Whatever it is, just do it. Rediscover what you love to do. You'll find that you've still got it and that it will bring you back to life from a zombie existence. It will also make you smile, and you will be nicer to yourself and others. That's the beauty of it.

Where's my spatula? I'm gonna be a-rockin' and a-rollin' in my garage thursday nights, and anyone is welcome to join in.

Midlife Rock Stars Rule!

Find Meaning in Life

"Let your suffering have meaning."
Abraham Lincoln

The day after she turned 40, my friend Betty decided to travel around the world in search of meaning in her life. She climbed the highest mountains, lived with the monks uninvited, went on a tree root diet, fed hungry wolves, and painted strange, unidentifiable objects, but she still couldn't find meaning in her life. When she finally came home, her 17-year-old daughter, who recently won an essay contest on the topic of abandonment, ran away from home. Betty's frantic, desperate search for her daughter ended up giving her the meaning she so craved. Sometimes, our meaning is closer to us than we realize.

Finding meaning in life is the mother lode of a midlife crisis. This is the missing link. This is what we are truly looking for whether we know it or not, whether we want to know it or not. It is the bridge to the second half of our life. Finding meaning doesn't have to be extravagant. You don't have to travel to the ends of the earth. The answer is within you. All you have to do is open your eyes and heart, dig a little, and bring it out.

A lot of people believe material things give them meaning. But they are misled, or they are lying to themselves and betraying their own truth. No amount of sports cars, cash, or jewelry can give you real meaning. Money could be the means to find meaning, but it isn't everything. A while ago, I heard a very famous celebrity say that the acting, the fame, and the millions of dollars were "not enough anymore." So, he ventured to find a cause that focused on something and someone else. He wanted to do something more "meaningful." Perhaps, if we started doing meaningful things early on, we wouldn't go through a midlife crisis.

In the first half of our lives, we were busy achieving our basic human needs such as shelter, food, and clothing. Then, as we approach midlife, we develop a higher, greater, innate need to give our lives purpose and meaning. We need a reason to get out of bed beyond work and paying bills. It's a need that is hard to ignore, but many people do it every day, prolonging their misery with absence of meaning in their perpetually empty lives.

Start with a simple acknowledgement. Say to yourself, "I am going to look for meaning in my life." Then have an attitude about it. How we look at things can influence how we see and act. Searching for meaning doesn't have to be profound, dramatic, loud, radical, or life-altering. It rarely is. In other words, you don't have to flip your life around. It's more of a realization of your true self and a need to fulfill a purpose in you. Take small steps and give yourself plenty of time, patience, and compassion to discover your meaning and incorporate it into your daily existence.

A meaningful life usually involves a passionate, dedicated, unselfish act that connects you to others directly or indirectly by giving them joy and love of some kind. And it all comes from an inner source, deep from the well of your being. We are much more than body and physical existence, you know. We want and need to make a difference and connect with something deeper that we can be proud of. Having meaning also validates our life. It says, "I was here. I made my mark. It wasn't all for nothing. My life meant something."

Only you can find and define meaning in your own life. There's no right or wrong here. There's only your truth. Through the years, your meaning might have gotten buried under a lot of manipulation, conditioning, and societal chaos, but it's still there, alive and well inside of you. You just have to listen to your inner voice to guide you and then dive into a sacred place in your heart and soul. Trust your gut. Trust yourself. There lies the passion, the wisdom, the compassion, and the much-needed and deserved serenity.

Remember, a genuine purpose gives life meaning. It's not a purpose to make money or to achieve status, but one that truly benefits yourself and others in need. Whether it's your 12-year-old son, a lost cause, a fight for the dolphins, or playing your old guitar on the street, it will comfort many souls, especially your own. And when this happens, it will automatically make your life twice as rich, and then, of course, you'll feel happy.

When we have meaning in our lives, growing old or sad things won't matter as much. *Who knew?*

We're way ahead, you know. So go for it. We are the lucky ones.

There Are No Answers Here.
Go Outside and Play Instead

"Loosen your girdle and let'er fly!"
"Babe" Didrikson Zaharias

I used to ask a lot of "why" questions. It annoyed everyone, including myself.

Why do I have to go to school? Why is the sky blue? Why is my teacher so mean? Why did the bully become a CEO? Why do people lie? Why do people die? Why are there so many idiots in this world? Why am I short? Why can't I eat whatever I want and still be thin? Why do bad people get away with everything? Why did I wake up with an extra thigh in the morning? Why won't Prince Charming ask for directions?! And the biggie, why is there so much suffering in this world? *Why, why, why, why, why, why?*

Finally at 40, I got exhausted. Both from asking the "why" questions, AND never getting an answer. That's when I discovered the truth. There are few answers here, so it's better to go outside and play instead. Unless you're a scientist, it's better to simply accept things we have absolutely no control over. There's a lot of those out there in our daily lives. That also includes some people. They don't make a lot of sense. So, instead of waiting for someone else to answer, I find and create the answer myself. Did you know you can do that?

Now, instead of asking, "Why is there so much suffering in the world?" I go and do something helpful to someone, and that becomes an answer for me. So, instead of waiting for the universe to send me a letter, an email, or a text, which could take millions of years or an eternity, I take control and take action with what I know and things that make sense.

In the movie "Unfinished Life," a character played by Morgan Freeman says, *"I had a dream that I flew last night. I was flying so high the blue turned to black. Up there, I saw everything, and it seemed there was a reason for everything."*

I have no doubt there is a reason for everything, but we human beings cannot see it, or we're not allowed to understand it here on Earth, and I'm sure there's a reason for that, too. So don't ask. Just be in the present moment and enjoy what you have and what you do understand. Don't waste any more time and your precious energy looking for answers that are not really there.

Part of growing older, wiser, and more mature is to come to terms with the way things are in our world and in the universe. It doesn't mean anything bad or negative. You are simply accepting life as it is with few questions, and enjoying what you do have and what you can do, rather than what you can't. *Capiche?*

Spend your time with what you are certain of, such as the love of your family, friends, making a difference, singing a song, strumming a guitar, helping a neighbor, feeding a hungry puppy, reading a really good book under a majestic tree, diving into a really good piece of chocolate cake, and keeping a dream alive.

I don't ask "why" questions any more. As a matter of fact, I avoid the word as much as possible. I figure the answers will all unveil themselves when it's time. But for now, I'm happy to go outside and play.

Become a Party Animal

"Live today. Plan for tomorrow.
Party tonight."
Anand Singh

My parents are known as "Party Animals." They are both in their 80s and they still work full-time. But this doesn't stop them from partying like 18-years-olds. Twice a month, they go and play 18 holes of golf. My father has dozens of trophies from coming in first or second place. He beats out younger players, who are in their prime physically. And my mother has made not one, but two holes-in-one, without even trying. People call them day and night to take them out for breakfast, lunch, and dinner. They're always getting gifts as well, from a box of pears or chocolates to seaweed and makeup. Everybody wants to hang out with the party animals. They are extremely popular, because they are genuine and fun to be with and have so much life.

To this day, no matter what happens, my father eats three square meals a day. Whether there's an earthquake, a riot, a bankruptcy, or a war, he sits down and eats his meal quietly and calmly. He says he wakes up hungry. That's another thing; my father wakes up at the same time every morning. He has for more than 80 years. It's really quite amazing. It doesn't matter how much or how little he slept the night before. The clock has nothing on him.

In addition to their hearty breakfast, the party animals cook a few days' worth of meals every day before heading out. They work together like a well-oiled machine. Being married to each other for more than 50 years has a tendency to do that. They hardly say anything. By 8a.m., they made enough healthy and delicious food to feed their kids, grandkids, neighbors, and friends.

Every morning, they go for a brisk walk around the neighborhood in matching sporty outfits. Then the party animals leave home around 9 o'clock in the morning and they seldom come back before 10p.m.Those are the days when there's nothing special going on. For lunch, they usually eat with their co-workers or friends.

And in the evening, they have to choose from an array of events, many from non-profit organizations, where they are board members or volunteers. In her 70's, my mother has served twice as the president of the largest Korean organization outside of Korea. She had to fight off age discrimination and sexism, but she never once gave up. My father has always stood by my mom as her ardent campaign manager and supporter. He himself served as president of his university alumni association for years. The two of them attend all kinds of meetings and fundraisers. They also volunteer at many places, including the senior center. They organize projects and raise money to help orphans, underprivileged children, domestic violence victims, and more. They believe in fighting for causes, especially the lost ones.

Even though they don't have to, they still work full-time. Half the money is given away for scholarships to young college students with financial needs, who are devoted to community service. They believe in helping young folks become future leaders to benefit the world, everywhere. My dad always says, "You make money so you can share it with others, and make a difference in the lives of those who were are less fortunate. Besides, you can't take it with you, so you might as well put it to good use while you can." Good point, Dad.

On the weekend, the party animals' schedule is dizzying. They play golf from dawn until dusk, and then they go out to dinner and pig out, followed by karaoke, where they each sing a dozen songs, shaking the tambourine and their booties with all the passion of rock stars. A few times a week, they go ballroom dancing too, where they do the cha cha, the Viennese waltz, and the tango. Then they head over to their favorite dive for a midnight snack or an early morning breakfast before heading home to get a few hours of sleep.

I struggle all day with seven hours of sleep and I'm always tired on top of that. My parents jump out of bed with more energy than 20 year olds. I, on the other hand, have to hurl my body off the bed to wake up halfway. I'll never understand why I didn't inherit my parents' endless energy gene. I've been ripped off. I tell you!

In addition to being such great golfers, my parents are also amateur ballroom dance champions. Their basement and attic are filled with dance trophies. My father owns several dance outfits, and my mother has those wide, feathery dresses for doing all kinds of ballroom dance moves like Fred Astaire and Ginger Rogers. And the kids, the grandkids, and fans are always at their competitions, taking their pictures and cheering them on. They are unstoppable.

We once went on a cruise together and the band and the audience were so impressed with my parents' dancing that they asked if the party animals could give dance lessons. They ended up giving free dance lessons, judging a dance competition, and making loads of friends, who were grateful that they had so much fun on a really crappy cruise. It even reunited a couple on the verge of a break-up. Nobody wanted to get off the boat!

A few years ago, we attended a very stuffy fashion show at a small boutique . People were falling off their chairs out of boredom. I was one of them. Most of the attendees were White folks over 70 years old. And my parents' first language wasn't English. So there wasn't a lot of talking going on. Then they decided to communicate through another language. They asked the DJ to play some disco music and they started dancing right there between the clothes racks. They did the hustle, swing, and the mambo. Soon, my parents pulled the others in, and they all started dancing in a circle. The clothes racks got pushed to the back or thrown into the storage room, and the little carpeted boutique turned into a dance club. Everyone, I mean everyone, was boogieing down, including a couple in their 90s and a gentleman in a wheelchair. Nobody wanted to go home. In the end, everyone hugged each other and thanked my parents for turning a dull event to a night they won't forget. My parents became the most popular and adored couple of the event. It was amazing. They were my heroes. They were the coolest party animals.

At home, my parents can't stay still. My dad can still lift heavy objects with ease and fixes things all over the house with a hammer and a screwdriver, and my mother cooks up a storm for 8 hours straight on her feet. She's an incredible cook. When I tell my mom to rest, she says, "I can rest, do nothing, and sleep when I'm dead." Good point, Mom.

As you grow older, you might think you have to slow down. Why? Nothing could be further from the truth. You need to be more active, move more, and get into the groove. This will keep you younger, living longer, as well as prevent you from becoming a cranky old curmudgeon. No matter what your age is, you can still be useful and have fun. You can't sit in the rocking chair, at least not yet.

My parents don't have a lot of philosophies. They don't need them, because they are living their lives to the fullest. Their parents, from the old country in Korea, died in their 40s and 50s in horrible war-torn times. My parents also survived the horrors of wars: fleeing from their homes at young age, losing their parents, siblings, and friends to murder and torture. As soon as they were able to, my parents immigrated to America in search for a better life for their children. They suffered working long hours, enduring prejudice and discrimination, and all kinds of squalor to make ends meet and to educate and raise three children in a foreign country. I don't know how they did it. But they did pay a price, an enormous one.

My mom and dad feel they are truly blessed for every single day of their lives. They don't take it for granted. They see it as a gift, and they make sure they make each day useful, brilliant, and magnificent as possible. They never focus on dying or getting old. They would say, "What's the point in doing that?" They consider it an utter waste of time and energy, and they are too busy to think about it.

So become a party animal. Go out there and work, play, help, and party. It ain't over 'till it's over. Take it from my folks. Today, they're going to host an auction to raise money for underprivileged students, followed by a dance competition, and an all-night partying with great food, friends, and loads of laughter and LIFE! And I'm going with them. The genes are finally kicking in. I'm gonna be a party animal too. *Woohoo!*

Shoot For Wisdom, Not Botox

*"It is characteristic of wisdom
not to do desperate things."*
Henry David Thoreau

One of the greatest prizes for getting older is wisdom. Your life experience, especially the hard part, was not for nothing. Like wine, we age gracefully when we choose to welcome wisdom into our lives. It's our reward for having survived the first half of our hectic, crazy, and tough lives.

I've learned that wise people don't have some exclusive mystical formula sent from a higher power. They simply pay attention to their life experience, lessons learned throughout their lives, and their hearts and soul. They listen to themselves. Monks, gurus, and priests are not the only beings who become wise. We all can as well. Each one of us has the ability and the source within us.

According to experts, wisdom comes from suffering, compassion, life experience, time, age, and an open mind and heart. When you experience losses and heartaches, you are expanding your realm of understanding. In other words, you understand someone else's pain because you've been there. That's the connection. Wisdom is to accept and to share what you know and what you have acquired from being human for more than 40 years. Wisdom is the gift for having walked thus far weathering everything from storms to surprises in every direction. So accept it. You've earned it.

I always find it horribly tragic when I see older folks full of bitterness and hatred. They didn't learn the most important thing from living. What was the point in getting old? What a waste. To me, the one person who captures wisdom so well is his Holiness the Dalai Lama. I'm not a Buddhist and I'm not from Tibet, and I'm not related to Richard Gere, but the Dalai Lama personifies wisdom in the truest form. He doesn't claim to be wise but he lives it. I really like that. Being wise means you've acknowledged your life experience and have compassion for yourself and others. You are empathetic and accepting of people and things with kindness and love. When you feel a sense of wisdom, the unknown or the mysterious no longer threatens you. And that could be your Uncle Bob! You accept things as they are and look for the beauty and the light instead of the darkness.

I can finally feel my own wisdom. And it didn't come from volumes of books or a doctoral degree. It came from my life experience, the good and the bad. It also came in giving to others. Making a difference in someone else's life gave me compassion and self-respect, and it eventually led to good ol' wisdom. That's how it works. You can't sit around saying you are wise. You have to act, reach out, and help. Wisdom is action.

Just imagine you have the power to make a difference in somebody's life right now. Did you know you were that powerful? And the rewards are numerous. One of them is your wisdom, which in return gives you a sense of self-worth, calmness, inner peace, and a balance with you and the infinite universe. I'd say that's a pretty good deal, wouldn't you?

Don't Take Life and Yourself So Seriously

*"Do the best you can,
and don't take life too serious."*
Will Rogers

Jonathan was a very serious man. He had a serious job and a serious house in a serious neighborhood. He wore a serious suit and carried a serious briefcase all the time, everywhere. All his things were serious, including his books, movies, magazines, furniture, paintings, and even his pots and pans. He loved serious entertainment and serious food. He hung out only with serious people doing serious things. And when he decided to adopt a dog from an animal shelter, he looked for the most serious dog on the planet.

Life was very serious for Jonathan. Everything was in perfect order, and it worked like a serious machine. Jonathan was seriously pleased. Then one day, while he was working on a serious case in his black and gray office, he collapsed and was institutionalized in a psychiatric hospital. Diagnosis? Jonathan had gone seriously mad. He couldn't stop giggling or laughing. And he got in trouble for playing practical jokes on his fellow psychotic patients and the nurses. His situation became very serious.

I met Jonathan for the first time on a blind date years ago, and you guessed it -- it was horribly serious. He showed up on the date wearing a black suit on a Saturday night, carrying an umbrella and a briefcase. We were meeting at a casual restaurant for appetizers and drinks on a hot night with most people wearing t-shirts and shorts. At first I thought he was an undertaker. He couldn't be my date. Wrong! As he introduced himself with a handshake and a business card, his face remained absolutely still. I'm not even sure if he ever blinked his eyes. For the next (really long!) hour, he alone talked about how serious dating was for him and how serious his woman had to be. I had only one thing on my mind: "How in the heck do I get out of this nightmare, YESTERDAY?!!" And how I was going to kill the person who set me up with this serious bozo?!

After awhile, I felt sorry for Jonathan. I mean, what kind of a life could this man have, taking himself and everything so seriously? How does he go through life without laughing? It had to be a separate hell. But he was still a bore. He couldn't relate to anyone who laughed. I did a few times to lighten things up during our one and only date, but he looked at me with a very displeased look, so I stopped. I was at a funeral. MINE! *Ughhhh...*

I asked my parents once or twice, "what is life?" They ended up giving me the best answer. They said, "Life is just life. We deal with what comes and goes and we do the best we can. The most important thing is not to take life so seriously or you'll miss it." You'll miss it. I wish I could have told that to Jonathan before he went mad.

We have a lot of serious things in our lives that we don't have any control over, so if we take everything else seriously on top of that, we can definitely go mad, one way or another. I'm sure you've seen people like this yourself.

Remember: Don't miss life by being so serious. Otherwise, you might end up like poor serious Jonathan. He's out of the institution now. He plays the piano at a local church and gives out free legal advice, and above all, he doesn't take too many things seriously, including himself. Thank goodness. He's never been so happy.

A Brief Thought on Blind Dates:

One time I dated a man named "Mr. Magoo." I kid you not. While he was bragging about what a wonderful catch he would be to any woman over an all you can eat buffet for $4.99, I was thinking, if I married this guy, I would be "Mrs. Magoo. Mrs. Clara Magoo!" His name was not the biggest problem. His arrogance, splitting the bill with a calculator, not tipping at all, and stealing the leftover in a ziploc bag under the table, and putting it into my purse, and asking me for bus fare kinda made me say "no thanks" to a second date.

Blind dates are guaranteed to be weird, not to mention absolutely ludicrous. Who could come up with this stuff?

Release Your Compassion Already!

*"Love and compassion are necessities,
not luxuries. Without them humanity
cannot survive."*
Dalai Lama

When 9/11 happened, I was in my office glued to my little TV set. Everyone on the entire floor came to see the tragedy unfold. Silently, each one of us started to shed tears as our hearts ripped with pain and agony. We didn't know anyone who died. They were complete strangers, but we were connected with their sorrow. This was our compassion in action.

We don't think about compassion too much these days. I mean, how many times does it come up in a conversation? But this unexpected and surprising healing method arrived during my midlife crisis, as I searched for meaning in my life. I was experiencing a disconnection with the world that often rejected me and left me in total isolation with a broken and lonely heart. However, being aware of my compassion and practicing it towards others and myself, I reconnected with the world, which led me to the path of wisdom and love.

Compassion is the ability to understand and feel the pain of others and an innate desire to help others wholeheartedly. Compassion also comes from suffering and life experiences. We cannot grow without suffering. We cannot relate to others without suffering. We need to transform suffering into insight and then insight into compassion. I can feel the pain of others because I've felt it too. The pain we share as human beings is what connects us, and we can comfort each other. It is what we have in common, what binds us together for life. Compassion also helps us to survive a lot of the pain in an often unjust and cruel world. When you approach the world with compassion, it's not as challenging, scary, or ugly. You begin to see hope and beauty in yourself and others.

Compassion is more than an act of kindness. It gives you self-confidence, and you feel good about yourself. So, you may look at it as giving to others, but you are also receiving at the same time. How brilliant is this? According to the Dalai Lama, when one has a sincere and open heart, one naturally feels self-worth and confidence, and there is no need to be fearful of others. However, a genuine change must first come from within the individual, and then he or she can attempt to make significant contributions to humanity. In other words, your compassion should include yourself as well. We are so good about forgetting ourselves, even though we are together from beginning to end. What's up with that?! You suffer too, you know. So exercise some compassion towards yourself, as well as others. You have enough heart and soul to go around.

Compassion and wisdom are tied together. Just like wisdom, compassion comes from giving to others, making a difference, and opening up our hearts, and expanding our scope of understanding beyond normalcy. It is the ability to connect heart to heart, soul to soul, and to simply help those who cannot make it alone during dark times. We've all been there. Without somebody's compassion and understanding, many of us would not be here.

Those who suppress their compassion could betray their own hearts and souls. When they deny the opportunity to express their compassion, they miss the full potential to love and be loved and to grow and become a wiser human soul. What a thing to miss! Don't deny yourself this great treasure.

You have this incredible power of compassion in you. Release it and show if off and let it take you to awesome places. You will never run out of it.

One Good Deed a Day

*"Goodness is the only investment
that never fails."*
Henry David Thoreau

Out of the blue, for no reason at all, I decided to do one good deed a day.

I remember helping someone by chance and I felt immensely happy and gratified in a subtle yet powerful way that carried me throughout the day. I ended up grinning all by myself. After some reflection, it turns out I was doing good deeds all along, but I didn't know it. So, from now on, I was going to do one good deed a day, consciously and validate it, because it just felt so darn good! And it was a great source of instant happy.

I didn't know it, but opportunities to do good deeds are everywhere in a given day. Most of us are oblivious to it. But when I choose to recognize it, it's all over the place. I didn't have to even look for it. It just came. It doesn't have to be grand like saving a life or the planet, which would be great if you can, but most of the time it's small, simple, easy stuff, that rarely requires much energy or tools. You are enough to help someone every day. *Isn't that amazing?!*

For example, I was on a tour of an animal rescue farm, and a guy came alone and he was desperately trying to take a selfie next to a thousand pound cow, but he struggled, dropping his phone, unable to get the right angle. So I offered to take the picture for him. Easy. Not only was he grateful, but elated that he took a picture with a beautiful and gentle cow. He proudly sent the picture to all his friends and he became the star of the day. He smiled and admired his picture the whole time. And best of all, he made a substantial donation to the rescue group. That was my one good deed of that day. *Yes!*

At the check-out at the grocery store, an elderly woman had trouble putting her food items on the conveyer belt because of severe arthritis. Both the cashier and the man behind her were rolling their eyes, tapping their fingers, and giving her full-blown rude attitude, which made her more nervous and near tears. So I offered to help and with both of my hands, I swooped all her items onto the counter. She was grateful beyond words. I told her not to worry and to not let those jerks get her down. Someday, I will be that old lady with arthritis and I hope someone will be there to offer me a helping hand to salvage some dignity with simple human kindness. It's not even hard.

While walking my dogs, I noticed a woman who had locked herself out of her house. While picking up her newspaper, the door closed on its own. It happens. In her jammies, bedroom slippers, and hair curlers (they still exist!), she was frantic, embarrassed, and panicking. I offered to help. I called her daughter on my cell phone and she came over and opened the door. Good deed! *Easy peasy*. And after I did it, I said to myself, "Good deed of the day." An inevitable and wide smile on my face naturally followed. It's a cool drink of self-satisfaction and happy. It doesn't cost anything and I get so much out of it. You've got to try it. If there's a magic potion to make you tingle with happiness, this is it. Sometimes, I do the happy dance after the good deed, but only when no one else is around.

I also give out compliments now. I've always kept them to myself, but it turns out people don't get enough of them. The first time I told a waitress that she was the best waitress I've ever had, she was blown away. She went into shock. She said people only complain, but rarely say anything nice. She said I made her day. Wow! I thank people out loud too, whether it's on the street, at work, on the road, etc. I say thank you and hello. I also wave to police officers, firefighters, city workers, gardeners, mail carriers, squirrels and crows, etc., in our neighborhood.

We live in a time when we don't acknowledge people any more. You could be standing or sitting next to them for hours, and not a single word or a glance gets exchanged. *Amazing.* We've become very good at acting like we are alone and we like it that way. And what happened to saying, "please?" It's gonna make a comeback. I also ask for people's names and make it a point to use them. You can't imagine the look on their faces when I remember their names. They are dumbfounded, as a barrier is shattered and it becomes easier to communicate, not to mention you get great service. *Win win!*

Some of the hardest people to be good to are families. You know exactly what I mean. So give yourself extra credit for doing a good deed for family members, especially those that seem annoying or poisonous. Doing a good deed really benefits you more than those receiving it. And it's not about getting anything back. *It's just because…*And it takes virtually nothing to do a good deed. Perhaps a little time, but that's it.

If helping people is frightening and you're not ready for it, there are always many animals, trees, the ocean, and plants in need of help. Give some water to a poor plant dying of thirst. Feed a hungry dog or a turtle. They are more grateful than you'll ever know. Animals are the most defenseless creatures on our planet, so give them some TLC whenever you can. I always carry some dog/cat food and water, just in case I see a stray. I could have the worst day possible, but if I've done one good deed, it turns it into a worthwhile day that wasn't a waste, and I am content.

Keep it simple. Open the door for someone, buy a cup of hot chocolate for a homeless guy outside, let someone in a hurry get ahead of you, pour some milk out for hungry cats. It will make you smile, be happy, and the endorphins will kick in right away. We all win.

I thank you in advance.

The Real Beginning

"In the midst of winter,
I found there was within me,
an invincible summer."
Albert Camus

A lot of people think midlife is the beginning of the end. I thought that too. After all, our body parts are starting to unravel, sag, wrinkle, and break down one by one. And for no reason, it hurts here and there, when we're not even moving. *What?!* It's shocking. *I hear ya!* But, it turns out that midlife is actually the real beginning of our true lives, the one we were meant to live, and the birth (not the death) of all the treasures that have been locked inside of us. It's an awakening of our inner self. It really all begins here.

In the first half of our lives, we lived by other people's rules. We had to live up to everyone's "shoulds." First it was our parents, then the teachers, peers, employers, nagging relatives, girlfriends and boyfriends, spouses, lovers, in-laws, and a few others in between. We were also a slave to culture, customs, traditions, rules, fashion, fads and trends in our society we had no part in making. We wore all the necessary masks to survive in our complex and imposing human world, and nodded our heads at the right time. Very little of it was our true selves. But we behaved, relatively.

It's understandable that in the midst of all the "shoulds," we forgot about our real self. After all, we had to pay the bills, study for exams, do chores, raise kids, go to the gym, take care of parents and weird relatives, be responsible, be a grown-up, wear the "right" clothes and drive the "right" cars, and try to get rid of wrinkles. But now, a voice is calling out. It's yours. And it's saying politely, "Let me out already!" It's time to listen to you.

Midlife is another transitional phase in our life's journey. Just like when we went from being a kid to a teen, a teen to a young adult, and so forth, this is another phase that changes and moves us forward. It's completely natural. And fighting nature usually doesn't look pretty and it is a losing battle and the price is high, physically, emotionally, and spiritually.

Like any phase in life's journey, it doesn't always happen quietly, painlessly, or without pimples or hot flashes. We humans also like to make things harder on ourselves. So we put up a fight to push it away by doing really strange and destructive things, like trying to be a 16 year old again, buying things we can't afford, and pulling our faces in every direction with chemicals and needles, just to mention a few. We don't like change and it scares us to death, so this is what we do. Wouldn't it be great if it worked? But it doesn't.

Ellen is 54 and she only shops and wears teen clothes, and blankets herself with as much bling as her tiny body can hold. The cheap and heavy makeup of blue eye shadow, blood red lipstick, and glitter is on her face 24/7. She pretends to like hip hop music and hangs out at the mall, smoking by herself, trying to look "cool." She doesn't get looks of admiration. She gets something else. Her exterior is the least of her problem. Do you know anyone like this?

At midlife, we need to pay attention to more than our bodies. We are made up of more than that. We also have a mind, heart, spirit, and a soul - all the good stuff. And in it lies some amazing treasures your creator gave you. One of the treasures is a set of survival tools to help us ease into midlife and beyond, to age gracefully, and to relish the wisdom that comes with new experiences, such as meaning and purpose. If you ignore all this, you will not only be an unhappy being in denial, but you'll miss an amazing opportunity to experience what you are truly made of, the whole shebang! It's like you have this wonderful house and you've only seen one room. It would be such a shame not to see and enjoy the rest of the house.

When you open yourself to the new possibilities, you start to see life truthfully, and not fear it as much. You'll see most of the good and less bad. This time it will be through your eyes and not someone else's. Then you will live a deeper, meaningful, spiritual, and greater life beyond material and tangible existence. You will live life according to YOU. *Imagine that.*

In midlife, youth is still there inside of you. As a matter of fact, it's just being born. So while your body is growing "mature," your inner self is just being born and it's at the infancy stage, ready to grow and shine with all its treasures. Your soul has awakened. It's time to unleash all your passions, desires and dreams, and live life with excitement and vigor.

Midlife is not about being over the hill, but being on top of it, so enjoy the view. You've climbed it and earned it. Look out, relax, breathe, create, shout, and have a blast!

Forgive for Your Sake

"Always forgive your enemies.
Nothing annoys them so much."
Oscar Wilde

A miracle occurred a few years ago.
I got a call from an old boyfriend from way back. A guy who lied, cheated, stole my money, and ran off with my car wanted to see me after 20 years. He said he had something to say. This was a real dilemma. It took me years to get over all the anger and heartbreak that went with a horrible relationship, and now, he wanted to see and tell me something, something important to my face. He pleaded. I asked myself over and over, "Should I?" Would you?

You know that wonderful dream where you see your ex-boyfriend, ex-husband, ex-wife, ex-girlfriend, ex-anything that treated you like crap, digging ditches for a living while you bask in true love and wealth? I love that dream. Anyway, that's not what happened.

We met at a coffee shop. I didn't have any expectations. But I was nervous, as well as curious. I wanted to see if I had become a "mature" person with time and age to handle this. To my surprise and disappointment, my ex-boyfriend looked well. *Darn.* He was wearing a suit and he was clean-cut and shaven. We shook hands and sat down, and he threw me a compliment or two to break the monumental tension. I think one of us also mentioned the weather. Then, after a very long silence, I politely asked him what he wanted to tell me. He took a couple of sips of his water, took a deep breath, and looked straight into my eyes and said:

"Clara, I just wanted to say I'm so sorry I hurt you. I was an absolute ass for lying to you, cheating on you, and stealing your stuff. It took me a long time to figure out why I did those things, especially to you. I know now that I was screwed up and I didn't like myself very much. And you made me feel things I didn't want to. I remember hearing you cry, but I pretended not to hear you. I didn't want to be in love with you, but I was and I tried to make you hate me. I was a real jerk and I

don't have any excuses. My biggest regret is that I hurt you. You didn't deserve that. You were so good to me. For that, I'll always consider myself lucky. I've wanted to tell you all this for a long time, but I didn't know how. Clara, I am truly, truly sorry and I hope that you can forgive me somehow."

I was dumbfounded. I froze. I couldn't blink, breathe, or pick up my jaw off the floor. This is when I wake up, right? Was this the same guy? And then I thought, "Is he dying? Does he have a fatal disease? Did he find Jesus?" When I asked gently, he chuckled and said, "No, I just wanted to make peace with you and myself." I froze again. This was not what I expected. It was the first and only time ever, a guy apologized for hurting me, let alone pleaded for my forgiveness. I didn't know what to do or what to say. Then he asked me again if I could forgive him. I gave him an honest answer: "I don't know." I honestly didn't know. I didn't want to just say the words. I wanted to truly forgive, for his sake and mine. So I ordered an apple pie ala mode and started thinking hard and fast.

Forgiving someone who caused me enormous pain was not easy. His cruelty damaged and changed the course of my life forever. I have the permanent scars to prove it. Forgiving him meant, I had to acknowledge the pain and anger and then let go -- truly let it all go, otherwise I would still have the resentment.

I knew that the act of forgiving is not an act of sacrifice or giving, but rather an act of gaining and empowering. It was an act of getting my life back and having control over it. When we forgive, we release the victim we held onto for so long. We release all the hostility, bitterness, and hatred that kept us from moving forward. As long as I didn't forgive him, I had an unhealthy connection to him, and I didn't want that any more.

Part of forgiving also meant coming to terms with the past, getting rid of excess baggage, taking care of unfinished business, and letting go of things that I did not have control over. Forgiveness releases us from the past that's riddled with painful memories, mistakes, regrets, and experiences that have imprisoned us emotionally for a long time.

I discovered that the past could not be changed, but I had the power to change how I thought about it. The past was no longer about bitterness and resentment. It was an experience to learn and grow from. I also decided to forgive, remembering that I hurt others too, unintentionally, and we all need to ask and receive forgiveness one way or another.

After I finished my pie, I finally said, "Yes, I forgive you as I forgive myself, too." Then we both felt a release, and then we chuckled and laughed, and my heartfelt light and free, as we both smiled. I thanked him for asking me for my forgiveness and I wished him well in his journeys. I walked out of the coffee shop with an indescribable satisfaction. I was feeling kinda good. *I mean, I felt damn good!*

Gratitude
Learn from the Trash People

"Gratitude is the sign of noble souls."
Aesop

The sun was going down slowly early Thursday evening when I went outside to walk my dog. That's when I saw them coming out in droves. I was amazed how many there were now. And, I could tell, it was a race for the plumpest bins.

They used to come out only after dark, when homeowners placed their green, blue and black trash bins on the sidewalk neatly the night before the official trash pickup day. No one knew trash people existed for a while, but sometimes we heard sounds of broken glass and tops of bins being shut noisily, as people with no faces, ragged clothes, and large shopping carts scurried away like rats before they were seen by human eyes.

Times have changed, even for the trash people. Today, as I turned a corner onto my favorite street with my dog, I saw them. At almost every house, someone was going through their blue and black bins. The blue ones were the most popular, because they had recyclable cans that could be turned into cash, or clothes that could keep them warm on chilly nights. The ones going through the truly dirty and smelly black trash bins, full of unimaginable filth and odor, were usually looking for food they could eat, rotten or otherwise. Once, I saw a man become suddenly elated to find a half-torn umbrella in a black bin on a rainy day. Some would find shoes, still with some miles left on them, but there were holes in the soles. Other things found in trash cans became ingenious inventions overnight that helped the trash people survive a harsh life.

Discovering usable trash was like hitting a jackpot to the trash people. They carefully put their treasure findings in their pockets full of holes or their overburdened carts. They put them there with joy, forgetting where the treasures came from. Pride was something they had to fold away in one of the trash bins long ago.

I was surprised to see that the trash people were of all ages and races now. It used to be mostly middle-aged men, who were at times intoxicated or delusional, looking for a bottle that wasn't completely empty or a cigarette butt that had some smoke left in it. They used to have dirty and long black beards and a face full of sickness of both the body and the soul. But it was a whole different story now. Poverty, survival, desperation, hunger, and bad luck knew no prejudice. It was all up for grabs.

As I continued to walk my dog with a heavy heart, I saw two young Hispanic girls with a perfect system of going through the blue bins. One would topple the bin while the other quickly separated the items into categories, then they had marked bags to put their findings in with great precision and speed.

Next to them was an Asian man in his late 50s wearing cheap sneakers and worn out shorts and a pair of glasses from the '60s that kept on sliding off his nose. He wasn't as fast as the girls, but he was diligent, and he went through every item, one by one. And then with respect, he put each item he did not want back in the trash bins. Then he wiped his hands, shook dust off of his cap, and moved onto the next house.

On the corner, I saw an elderly African American man. I'd seen him before. He was very polite. He would always say "hello," "please," and "thank you." He was much older and thus slower, and with aching joints and bones, he went through only one bin quietly, until it was too dark to see.

When the sun went down a little further, I saw a Caucasian man in his 30s with a goatee. He seemed new to the game. I could tell he was ashamed, as he looked around constantly in fear of being seen or recognized. He wore a relatively new baseball cap but he didn't fool anyone. I wondered if he was one of those tech-savvy guys who went bankrupt after a fast rise and fall in the computer business. One thing was clear: This guy knew a better life not so long ago.

But the worst was when I saw a child among the trash people. I froze with overwhelming sadness and despair. A small, thin child was clutching a dirty little rag doll, while holding onto her mother's sweater. Her mother had to get on her tippy toes to reach deep into the blue bin. She didn't find much down there, except some newspapers and a badly torn and faded handbag. People throw anything into the blue bins now. They don't bother to read what is recyclable. The mother took the handbag, dusted it off with her dirty hands. It was a gem to her. Her daughter was in awe, and she played with it for a while. I almost choked trying to hold back a flood of tears and anger, big enough to scare God himself.

Being a dog lover, it was equally heart-ripping when I saw an old man with a dog chained to his cart digging through the black bin. They both looked thin and obviously hungry. The dog was dirty. He probably never knew a bath or clean water, but I hoped he knew love from his unfortunate human friend. They didn't find much. So they moved across the street. The man was limping and he looked as if he was in a lot of pain. The dog followed without any choice, panting with the look of a wounded animal that was dealt a very poor hand in life. I looked at my dog, who was eyeing a squirrel. Before we left the house, he'd had a hearty dinner made of organic chicken and rice.

I had to stop. I didn't want to stare at the trash people, so I stayed at a distance and watched them in agonizing awe, and asked the question I had vowed never to ask in this lifetime, because I knew there was no answer here. But I couldn't help myself. It came over me like a shadow of a giant. *"Why, why, why do some people have more than others? Why?"*

Who are these people going through strangers' garbage bins day after day looking for soda cans, food, a drop of beer, or even a toy for their kids, and how did they become this way? Very few of them were drunk or wasted. They were sober, relatively young, and wore gloves, as they became professional trash diggers for survival. What could be going through their mind? Are they thinking anything? Or perhaps they didn't have the luxury to question anything? What are their stories? How did it come to this? I wanted desperately to know, and I wanted to run to them and ask, but I couldn't. I didn't want to offend them, and I was told they could even be dangerous, because they were desperate and scared beyond reason.

On the next block, the irony and the mystery of life were unfolding and my heart broke again. While the trash people continued digging through the bins, I saw a homeowner pull up in his driveway in a Mercedes sports car. The owner and the trash people didn't acknowledge each other. Either they were embarrassed, or worse, they didn't care. They each chose to be invisible. Across the street, a pizza was being delivered to a man who was too lazy to cook his own dinner. There were overweight joggers running around in their designer's sportswear while talking on their cell phones, and folks with their dogs like me, leisurely walking before a plentiful meal, which was waiting for them in a safe, clean, and warm home.

I walked slowly with a heavy sadness. My fellow man, woman, child, and dog were digging through fly, ant, and cockroach-infested trash bins to find a soda can that could get them a quarter or something edible, alongside alley cats. I could not fathom the experience of the trash people. To me, it was the ultimate human low.

I wanted to help them but I didn't know how. I could throw in more soda cans and extra goods in the trash bins, but it didn't seem to be enough. I wanted to hear their stories, but I could not go near them. I realized that in a blink of an eye, I too could end up as a trash person. We were not much different, as life has a tendency to be cruel and harsh without notice. So I hugged my dog and thanked God for being so blessed.

I gave one last look. Across the street, the trash people were too busy to notice my disappointment in the design of life and my heart that ached for their indignity. Why must life be so ugly, so humiliating, and so unforgiving?

It started to get dark, and one by one, they disappeared to a place I could not step into. I wondered where they were going, if they had a home or a family. I wanted to follow them, but it began to rain and I turned a corner and headed home. There, I skipped dinner and rummaged through the house and put extra soda cans, clothes and shoes, and my favorite teddy bear and other toys, along with a bag of dog treats, in my blue bin and wished them farewell and good mission. Unable to sleep, I spent the whole night staring out the window hoping that all the trash people, including that sweet but unlucky dog, were indoors somewhere warm and safe.

I had trouble sleeping that night. I was wrestling with myself. So I walked to the kitchen for a snack, even though I wasn't hungry. Then I heard a noise outside. It was three in the morning. I pulled the curtains back slowly and saw someone on the corner of the street opening a blue bin filled with empty bottles, broken glass, and torn newspapers. He was not alone. Beside him was a short woman who picked up everything he tossed out, while holding a broken umbrella over his head. In her right arm sat a small kitten.

It started to rain harder and tears rolled down my face one after another. Then, like the end of a movie, all faded to black, and soon I saw nothing but the deep darkness of the night. I closed the curtain slowly and headed for bed. There for the first time in a long time, I got on my knees to say a prayer, to simply say thank you for all I have and to please help the trash people and animals, whom he might have forgotten. *Please....*

For a long time, I was really good at complaining. I was famous for it. There was always something missing or wrong with my life. Then the trash people taught me a precious lesson: There is always someone who has less than I do. I saw it. I felt it. It cured my self-pity. When I need a reminder, I don't have to go far to see men, women, children, and animals that are hungry, cold, sick, hurt, alone, and scared.

Gratitude has long been associated with health, longevity, and happiness. When we focus on all that we have, we get a sense of appreciation, calmness, and happiness, which helps us steer away from desperate acts, which could get us in trouble. So make a daily list of things and people you are grateful for. I carry my list with me everywhere I go and use it both as a reminder and a tool when I succumb to feeling sorry for myself. There's no need for that, ever.

My mom used to say, "Look at what you have instead of what you don't have." Yes, mom. I know I have more than I know. Thank you.

Dealing with Difficult People
a.k.a. Idiots, morons, jerks, flakes, and yahoos

"Some people. What was God thinking?"
Unknown

Unfortunately, each of us has a set of annoying people in our lives -- real pests. Most of the time, we don't really know why they are there and how they came to be in our lives. But they're there. Some are close and others are not. Some we can get away from and some we have to live with. *Eek!*

Dealing with difficult and annoying people on a daily basis is probably one of the greatest stressors of all time. No doubt, some people can be a real pain in the derriere. However, we have to work with them, live with them, and be nice to them, which drives us to pull our own hair out, not to mention drink, cuss, kick, scream, and throw unknown objects across the lawn.

I used to let difficult people get under my skin. They bothered the crap out of me, and I responded brilliantly by stuffing my face with food at nights. I got fat, grouchy, and unhappy. I became a triple threat. So I had to find another way, a healthier and safer way. I knew this much: Annoying people will always be around, so what is the one thing I can do? What is in my power to do? Then the light bulb lit up. The answer was teflon. I needed to develop a teflon skin.

Teflon is a material nothing, I mean nothing, sticks to. Whatever lands on teflon just slides right off. So, see the faces of these annoying people, but don't let them stick to you emotionally or let them get under your skin and infect your whole existence. Don't give them that much power. Just let them roll off of you, even if it's for a little while.

Now in order to develop a teflon skin, you have to work on yourself. You can't change other people's behavior, but you can change how you perceive and react to them. If you become a secure, self-confident, compassionate, happy individual with a strong sense of self, these idiots and morons will not bother you as much. You will see them differently. Instead of being annoyed with them, you might even pity them. They simply won't matter as much because you like yourself. No one can shake you. You're wearing a teflon coat.

Here's another perspective. If someone bothers you a lot, it could be an issue about yourself. Unintentionally, some people could bring up hurtful and disturbing issues about yourself that you may not want to look at. So, discover what that is and face it.

My friend Martha, 42, loathed seniors. Every time she saw an elderly person, she'd chew them out and then run away with goose bumps, shaking her head in disgust. She couldn't stand them. These poor seniors brought up one of Martha's greatest fears: growing old. So we talked about it. Why she was afraid of growing old? What bad experiences she had with them? What could we do to alleviate her fear? After processing her issues, she didn't detest senior citizens any more.

We have a tendency to project our issues onto others instead of facing them ourselves, because they're too painful to look at. But they rarely go away by themselves. The only way to get rid of them is to confront them. It's not as hard as you may think, and you don't have to do it alone. So take a moment and see what the real issue could be.

Here's another idea. How about practicing kindness? Practicing kindness with jerks, you say? Are you mad?! I know. But you know what? It's better than the alternative and you get the most out of it. Does that make sense? Let me explain.

In the beginning, I resisted. It felt unnatural, but once I did it, it was very effective. You've heard of the saying, "Kill them with kindness?" Well, it's true. It works on most people and you benefit the most by not allowing difficult people to ruffle your feathers. It's not about their response, but your effort. Besides, they might have issues of their own that lead to their nasty and unlikable attitude. So try being kind and understanding to an irritating relative or an idiotic coworker. It will drive them nuts with confusion and perhaps bug the hell out of them, and you can walk away with a grin of joy and satisfaction. They might even appreciate it and change their behavior from negative to positive, and even be grateful. One can hope. Give it a go.

Then there are just plain ol' annoying people you cannot stand because they are loud, rude, arrogant, selfish, and shallow. Plenty of them around, I'm afraid. There are also people you just don't like for no reason. And you don't have to have a reason. There's no law that says you have to like everybody. Try to avoid these people as much as possible. They are what they are, but you now have the power not to let them get to you.

When someone is being difficult, it could also mean they are suffering deeply and are in a lot of pain from unresolved anger or fears. They could have serious issues and it might be repressed in their unconscious mind, which can manifest itself into abnormal behavior. Sadly, this is common. A lot of people carry their garbage around and dump it onto innocent people every day on the street, at work, on the freeway, cutting you off, yelling, screaming, etc. According to Thich Nhat Hanh, a Buddhist philosopher, when someone suffers, one could become extremely bitter. We've all encountered people who are always complaining, criticizing, and blaming others for their problems. They are truly unhappy folks. Most likely, they don't like themselves, so how could they like others?

Don't forget we have an advantage in midlife, because we can now recognize a flake or a jerk right away. We don't have to spend a lot of time giving them our money, hearts, or souls like we did when we were young. We are now experienced human beings, and we have the ability to tell the good from the bad. This isn't high school any more. We don't need to be popular or validated by anyone except ourselves.

There's one more thing. Try not to be a difficult person yourself. In other words, don't be a jerk, an idiot, and so on. If you are, you'll naturally attract them and lose good folks while you're at it. So work on not being a difficult person. Learn to be the kind of person you want to be with and they'll come flocking to you.

At this point in your life, there's absolutely no reason why so many negative and toxic people should be in your life and in your phone book, poisoning your well-being in every way. Distance yourself from those that are difficult as much as possible. Life is short and your energy and time are precious. It's reserved for the real folks.

And for those you cannot avoid, remember to wear a teflon coat. Wear it well. It comes with a lifetime warranty.

Warning:
According to EWG (Environmental Working Group), US Environmental Protection Agency, and other sources, non stick pots and pans, such as teflon can be hazarduous at high temperature. So, opt to use stainless steel or cast iron as a safer alternative to your health, environment, and wildlife.

Spirituality
It's Time for a Little Soul Work

> *"Diseases of the soul are more dangerous*
> *and more numerous than those of the body."*
> Cicero

Have you talked to your soul lately?

You have one you know. To my surprise, spirituality became a powerful healing method that soothed my neurotic midlife crisis, depression, and cancer, among other things. I didn't know it, but I was suffering from a spiritual starvation. I totally neglected my soul. But once I had some soul food, spirituality gave me a sense of belonging, acceptance, and inner calmness I desperately needed. Life and growing older didn't scare me so much.

Why do we need spirituality?

In addition to our physical, emotional, and social needs, we develop a need to understand where we are going, where we belong, what life is all about. We yearn for a greater spiritual connection, especially in midlife when we look for something deeper to give our existence meaning and to understand change, loss, aging, and death.

Spirituality rises above reality.

Life is tough and reality is harsh, so we seek something beyond ourselves that can soothe our souls when we are feeling unbalanced and weary. Spirituality heals us so that we can exist in a world that is often complex, mysterious, cruel, and completely nuts! It prevents us from being jaded with a hardened soul. It gives us a sense of wholeness and acceptance just as we are: flaws, scars, warts and all. Spirituality is something beyond us that is eternal, just, and kind; a hope beyond this world that is often full of despair and injustice. Spirituality gives us peace and a sense of hope and the possibility that perhaps all our suffering has a reason, a darn good reason.

Spirituality is also something sacred and divine. It gives us comfort in a world that often rejects and labels us as "worthless" or "different" or "old." Spirituality gives us a safe place to belong, as well as a perspective that is larger and greater than the human existence, beyond human control and human comprehension. I really like that.

Spirituality doesn't have to be in the form of a religion. Each person is capable of finding a sense of belonging and peace with himself or herself, as well as the universe. It's as unique as the individuals on Earth. The most important thing is to define it according to your true self, your true beliefs. For example, my friend Katie finds spirituality in sitting in a small chapel alone. Norbert finds it sitting at the top of a mountain he climbed, and Alice finds it in taking long serene walks in the woods with her dogs. Frances finds it in angels, Maggie finds it in the Buddhist temple buried in a deep cave in Asia, Harry finds it in the stars up above, and Julie finds it in the faces of homeless children she bakes cookies for.

For me, spirituality came from a combination of things such as finding a cause greater than myself and in helping others, instead of drowning in the cesspool of self-pity, as well as in nature, where I find beauty, unbelievable awe, fascination, serenity, and acceptance. I've also discovered that spirituality comes from a connection with people, as well as a higher being. With spirituality, I began to become a whole person. And, it all began with me, the individual.

Define your own spirituality. It comes from within your soul. So have a talk with it and do a little soul work. You'll be amazed at what you'll find.

Death
It's in Our Universe Now

"Dream like you'll live forever;
live like you'll die tomorrow."
James Dean

The last thing Ajumma does before she goes to bed every night is put on clean underwear and pajamas she won't be ashamed of. She can't go to sleep otherwise. She also makes sure her house is thoroughly clean and neat from top to bottom. Because, you see, she might not wake up in the morning. And the last thing she wants at the end of her life is to be accused of being old and dirty.

Ajumma is 86 years old. Like most people in their senior years, she has all kinds of health problems. She's broken her hips twice, has severe arthritis, walks with a cane, has high cholesterol and blood pressure, and the cancer is in remission, for the second time.

Death has been on her doorstep a few times, but it's never frightened Ajumma. It never has. "What is there to be afraid of?" she says. "It's just the end of life. I don't really know where I'll go, but I suppose that will be taken care of. I don't give it much thought. I have too much to do while I'm alive."

Ajumma was a dedicated Buddhist most of her life. But when her son was dying of stomach cancer at the age of 34, he asked her to convert to Christianity, and so she did. It was her only child's dying wish and the only thing she could do for him. So now she goes to church every sunday and she is grateful for every little thing she has in her life. She's still a vegetarian and meditates twice a day, and sheds a few tears for her son whom she can no longer embrace, but Ajumma still considers herself to be truly blessed. To her, no one is luckier in this lifetime. This is what she truly believes.

After 40, we begin to feel our mortality. It starts to sink in that we will not be on this planet forever, and time is not on our side, and there is something unknown waiting to take us onto our next journey. It's called Mr. Death.

Death: It comes to all of us and it is a journey we must travel alone. We are born alone and we die alone. But I've discovered that death is really about living, because it reminds us how precious our time and life are here, especially the second half of our lives. Life is so fleeting. So don't ignore it or waste it being afraid of it. Live every second of your life. We have control over that. Remember, death is a journey as life is. The rest is up to the Gods.

I still picture Mr. Death as Robert Redford from an episode of "The Twilight Zone." Have you seen it? It's a story about an old woman who barricades herself in her tiny apartment to shut out Mr. Death. But in the end, she realized she wasted her life and missed out on living. Her life was already dead. Eventually, she surrenders herself peacefully and goes off with Mr. Death to the mysterious unknown. It ain't so scary to go off anywhere with Mr. Robert Redford. Okay, it can be any dreamboat of your generation. I'll be off with Mr. Gregory Peck. Thank you.

Death is about living and not about dying. This is what I've learned. So live while you are still here.

What's Wrong with My Age?

*"I'm at the age where food has taken the
place of sex in my life. In fact, I've just had
a mirror put over my kitchen table."*
Rodney Dangerfield

What's wrong with my age, I ask you? It's the perfect age to do just about everything without getting into trouble.

The most death-defying question for women: "How old are you?" I am 55. I am proud of it. I survived 55 years of life as a human being in a treacherous and often cruel world. And even though I have scars, bruises, and a shattered heart being held together by duct tape, I am still breathing, wishing, dreaming, and eating!!!!

I met a 50-year-old woman the other day. As I looked at her, I noticed she didn't have a single wrinkle on her face. In fact, her face never moved. She barely opened her mouth to drink her lunch through a straw, and she never blinked. I got scared. Was she the daughter of Frankenstein? It was worse. She had countless plastic surgeries, which pulled her face so tight she could no longer move it or feel it. Why would anybody do this to themselves?

We are like wine, but even better. Those lines on your face are your life experiences; they're your stories, your joys and losses, all your memories. So why would you want to erase them, stretch them out, or pump them with chemicals? It's such an insult to your life and to your one and only body and face.

I don't trust people over 40 without any wrinkles on their face. It tells me they don't like themselves, and they have dishonored their own life and the people in it. I'm proud of my wrinkles, crow's feet, unidentifiable spots, and laugh lines. It means I've lived, cried, and expressed myself, and above all else, I laughed like mad, and I'm gonna do more of it.

Our culture is notorious for being obsessed with youth. We are so arrogant that we think we can beat nature and stay young forever. We are supposed to be intelligent creatures, and yet this is how we think and act. Now, this is absolutely insane.

I looked at the mirror the other day and found a white hair in my eyebrow. My eyebrow!!! I screamed. What up?! I fainted. My dog came by and sat next to me and waited.

When a woman discovers a gray hair in America, she freaks out and runs to get her hair colored darker than her natural color, which she can't remember, and then she runs to tell a shrink about it for $200 an hour. It becomes a life and death situation. Is it really? God forbid something natural should happen. Can you think of a thing or two that might be more important in life?

When a woman discovers gray hair in Botswana, she feels excitement and the whole family celebrates her good luck. In Korea, age brings you prestige and honor in society. You are considered wise, knowledgeable, and gracious. People bow to the older folks and speak and respond in a formal language out of respect. The elderly are considered superior. In Japan, a person cannot be the master of any art until they are at least middle-aged. Old age is associated with wisdom, a lifetime of knowledge, and experience. The Venda-speaking people of southern Africa also welcome wrinkles and old age as these signify the approaching contact with the real world of the spirits. *How cool is that?*

Staying truly "young" and slowing down the aging process is a combination of body, mind, and soul work. People who are physically healthy with emotional stability, open and calm minds, and optimism, not only have longevity, but vibrant lives. In other words, *they're really living, baby*!

Your body may age, but your mind, spirit, and soul are just awakening and being born, as I've mentioned before. Your whole being doesn't consist only of your body. That's just one aspect of it. You also have a mind, heart, spirit, and soul that will keep your body thriving. When you balance it all, this makes you a whole person, which will truly make you look and feel young, have a peace of mind, a great sense of self, and a giant grin on your face. *Ah....*

Aging is not a bad thing, as so many people try to sell us. It's part of life and it's natural and there's great beauty and grace in it. Don't rob yourself of that. So smile and let your life shine on your glorious face.

Get Over Yourself & Find a Cause

*"The least I can do is speak out for
those who cannot for themselves."*
Jane Goodall

We thought we had the formula for happiness.
We'd go to school, work hard, make a lot of money, fall in love and marry, and accumulate a lot of stuff. Then, and only then, we would be happy, loved, and successful, forever. *If only.*

Henry came into therapy with an entourage and a lot of stuff. I was told he was very rich and powerful and that he always got his way. *Okay.* However, before we got started, I had to explain to Henry that his entourage had to wait outside, along with his poodles, German shepherds, and Chihuahuas, ice bucket of champagne and Russian caviar, six ringing cell phones, laptops, and his manicurist. He didn't like my humble request.

Henry had money, power, people, attitude, and full-blown arrogance. But the first thing he said to me was, "I want to jump off a bridge every second of the day. I hate my life. I hate myself. Do something about it!" Henry had two Ph.D.s, a couple of hundred million dollars, several ex-wives, countless children, a few grandchildren, pets, cars, boats, buildings, clothes, antiques, paintings, and other stuff he'd lost track of. None of that mattered. He just wanted to jump off a bridge. I was seriously thinking, *"Who referred me to this guy?"*

Even though it's been proven a gazillion times -- historically, scientifically, and personally -- that money and things don't make us happy, we go after them every day. There's a new generation believing and doing the same thing. They just have to find out for themselves.

It's okay to go after money and some stuff, but you also have to go after a few other things to balance your life to find true happiness. I've learned that life is really a balancing act. If you're good at walking the tightrope with a long horizontal pole, you'll ace life. It turns out we have to balance both the external and internal things. Whenever you have too much of one thing, you will naturally get off balance. That's simple enough.

By midlife, most of us know all about the external stuff and how to get it. But nobody told us about the internal stuff we need, such as inner peace, a calm mind, wisdom, compassion, self-esteem, and spirituality.

When we only go after the external stuff, it's always about you, you, and more you. It's hard to believe, but that gets old and boring. The internal stuff works the other way. It's about somebody else, which become a part of you.

It's time. You need to get over yourself and find a cause greater than yourself. And, oh my goodness, you get so much back in return. You'll be blown away. It's kind of neat, really. When you stop thinking about only you, the rest falls into place. However, it has to be from a genuine place. You can't fake it, buy it, or hire somebody to do it for you. It has to be real and by wonderful you.

I learned this lesson late in life. When you give to others, you truly give to yourself. And the only way you can experience this is to do it yourself. If you want to increase your self-esteem, feel powerful, make friends, and feel and look young, go and volunteer and help someone else. There are millions of causes, millions of ways.

Mira, a former science teacher, became homebound in her mid-50s due to a medical condition. The first few years, she moped around feeling sorry for herself and biting her poor husband's head off. She felt worthless and useless. That's a double whammy. Then one day she saw some kids playing outside her house. Their parents worked long hours and they were alone most of the time after dark and on weekends. It looked like the kids were trying to get a paper rocket to fly. They didn't have a clue. So her husband invited them over and before you knew it, Mira was unstoppable. Science and kids were up her alley. The kids ended up winning first prize at a local science fair that year.

Today, kids gather in her backyard every friday night to see stars, comets, and galaxies up in the sky and talk about anything from microorganisms to aliens, over cookies and hot chocolate. Everybody has a good time learning a thing or two. Mira even helps kids get science scholarships.

Mira doesn't bite her husband's head off any more, and she isn't drowning in self-pity. She feels useful and worthwhile. Her life has meaning. She's giving to the kids, and they are giving her life back. Now that's a smart deal. Everybody can use some of this. It's funny how the body and mind are so closely connected. A few months ago, Mira's doctor told her she could go back to teaching. She wasn't sick or in pain any more. She didn't need the numerous medication she depended on for years for painful symptoms. No one can explain why -- or perhaps we can. The important thing is her spirit is soaring unbelievably high, and she's healthy, and her life is now about someone and something else. But guess who is benefiting the most? You guessed it.

My Treatment for Henry

In the meanwhile, we hosed down Henry of his make-up, bling-bling, fake hairpieces, puffy and glittering outfits, and put him in an ordinary shirt, a pair of jeans, and sneakers. He then went and volunteered at a local convalescent home a few hours a week. He went alone without his entourage. At first, he put up his dukes and all the defenses that went with it out of habit, but eventually he loved it. As a matter of fact, he ended up adopting a few grandmothers. It turns out Henry never had parents, and he was thrilled to be heard and be adored by dozens of parents. He became the senior center's surrogate son. Henry now owns the convalescent home, and added an extra wing and upgraded it to a resort level, but no one there knows about it.

He still volunteers there every Tuesday and Thursday, while his entourage does makeovers for the seniors, giving manicures and massages. Oh, the dogs are helping out, too. All they have to do is sit there and be who they are: sweet, cute, loving, and gorgeous dogs. Everybody is calm and happy enough to skip a few meds for a day. Happily, Henry graduated from therapy.

You have this incredible power you have not tapped into. You can't use it when you're dead, so what are you waiting for? Find a cause greater than yourself. Be useful to someone other than YOU and give a little, and you'll get a mountain of magic right back.

By the way, giving to a cause greater than yourself works wonders for broken hearts too. The next time you breakup, feel abandoned or disappointed, go ahead and listen to sad love songs, swallow a box of chocolates, and sob during sad and happy commercials for a little while, and then go out and volunteer, and simply help someone else. I found this to be the best cure for broken hearts, or broken anything.

When you remove the spotlight from yourself, you'll find that your problems are not the greatest in the world. There are always others who are worse off than you, and you have the power to ease someone else's pain. This will get you out of your head and your house. You'll connect with others. And while you are helping, you could begin to heal from your own ailments, body and mind. So, get over yourself and let your compassion explode for the greater good. Everyone will thank you.

Henry was so happy, he offered to buy me a boat. I settled for a box of chocolates instead. I know. *Dumb, but happy.*

Love & Soul mates

> *"Grow old along with me;*
> *the best is yet to be."*
> *Robert Browning*

When a reporter asked Audrey Hepburn what was the most meaningful relationship she had with a man in her life, she didn't mention her husbands or any of her famous Hollywood co-stars. Instead, she talked about a man she never married but cared for with deep passion, respect, love, and undying friendship in her later years. She said he was "her spiritual twin," the man she wanted to grow old with.

In the second half of our lives, we want a relationship that is meaningful and long- lasting. We want companionship. We already did everything foolish, crazy, stupid, and moronic with our bodies and hearts the first half. Now, it's time to settle down a bit. It's about finding a soul mate. This time, it's about sitting with someone and being comfortable not saying a word. It's about being with someone who understands you without explanations, graphs, or maps. It's not about how you look, but how you carry yourself. It's a connection from heart to heart and soul to soul. It's about respect and understanding that equals love.

There's no need for a legal piece of paper to prove your love any more. Thank goodness for that. There's no pressure to tie the knot or to have children. There is only the two of you, friends and lovers till the very end. When I run into an elderly couple holding hands, I often ask them what their secret is to a long and happy relationship. They all say the same thing: friendship, respect, love, and, oh yeah, great sex!

So don't miss out on finding your soul mate by looking in the wrong place, focusing on the external rather than the internal. You don't want to grow old alone, or worse, become an old geezer hitting on young women or men at a bar all by yourself. *Ew…*

Make time for finding and keeping your soul mate. Whether you end up alone or not is mostly up to you. Remember, the night is young, and we are middle-aged and anything, I mean anything, can happen. *Ooh la la.*

Angry? *Pissed Off?*

"When angry, count to four.
When very angry, swear."
Mark Twain

I think being angry is one of the most natural states for a human being to be in, given the insane design of life. Just think of what you had to do in your life or just this morning.

I bet you juggled a dozen errands, worked out, fought traffic, squeezed into a tight suit, put your make-up on in nine seconds, made conference calls, checked your endless emails, and dealt with nasty office politics all before your first cup of coffee. As a mom, you made a power breakfast to feed an army, speed-drove your kids and dropped them off at five different schools, did a mountain of dishes, started the laundry, cleaned crap off the walls and floors, walked the dogs, ran to the gym, washed the car, picked up the dry cleaning, and patiently listened to your mother-in-law complain about your "little weight problem," all before heading over to three different markets, carrying coupons, babies, and bags. And then, it was time to make dinner.

As a woman, I am expected to be smart, pretty, thin, young forever, cute, sexy, submissive, assertive, obedient, and a brilliant cook, every single day. That reminds me of a card I got that said, "Ginger Rogers did everything Fred Astaire did, but backwards and in high heels." Got that right! It's actually quite amazing what we do every day, and *what* and *who* we put up with. Give yourself a standing ovation and a pat on the back. You've earned it, and then some.

My family and I left our mother country, South Korea, to escape the threat of war and communism and immigrated to a whole different country, leaving behind our relatives, friends, and our identity forever. Nothing would be the same. Everything had to change.

My parents worked 16-18 hours a day, seven days a week, cooking, cleaning, scrubbing, waiting on customers, and washing dirty dishes. They had to put up with blatant discrimination, thugs that tried to extort money, and thieves of all kind. We had to learn a whole different language and adapt to a new culture, which wasn't always kind or inviting. Often, we were labeled inferior because of our skin color and the shape of our eyes. How silly is that?! Kids used to throw tomatoes at me and beat me up because I wasn't White. I've dealt with racism and discrimination since I was a kid, and I know I'll have to deal with it for the rest of my life. Now that is infuriating.

Crap happens to us all the time. Dealing with life issues beyond our control, unforeseen tragedies and illness, as well as working and living with morons, idiots, and bad guys every hour on the hour is absolutely maddening. The worst part is that we are constantly told to "take it" or "live with it" or "accept it." So it makes sense that we are pissed off sometimes. *Sometimes?*

An expert on anger said the main reason most people are angry is due to injustice. People feel life is unfair and they have no right or a voice, and they end up taking it all. I know what that's like. Just the other day, someone yelled that I should go back to where I came from. A restaurant hostess refused to give me a table by the window because I wasn't young, and I lost count on how many times I got ripped off. It's all over the place. Even though you do all the right things, life can spit in your face. No doubt. All of it can be maddening and we don't know what to do with it. After all, we still have to survive and live, but it's hard when we are beaten up a lot. No wonder some people go ballistic.

Anger, especially pent-up anger, can lead to anxiety, nervousness, tension, panic attacks, self-defeating behaviors and twitching eyelids. It can also lead to drug and alcohol abuse, depression, suicide, self-hatred, stress, high blood pressure, physical and emotional abuse, diseases, crime, and CONSTIPATION! It also ages us fast. And it hurts those we love, so we need to find a way to deal with it before it spins out of control.

Anger often comes from disappointment, feeling powerless, hopelessness, rejection, criticism, fear, a lack of control, insecurity, fear, frustration, and loss. Did I leave anything out? It's even worse for women. We were taught and told to suppress anger. Angry women were seen as unladylike, not feminine, and impolite. St. John's University in New York conducted research to develop a new anger disorder scale, which showed that women were angry longer, more resentful, and less likely to express their anger. Men were traditionally encouraged to be overt with their anger.

Here's what has worked for me when dealing with anger. Have you looked at your face when you're angry? I did. Once when I was truly pissed off, I froze my expression and ran to the nearest mirror. It was horrifying. My angry face was ugly, contorted, and scary. My mom once told me that my face could get stuck there and it would stay mean and ugly forever. And I think she was right. For some people it has. Have you noticed the faces of people who are always angry or cranky? It's completely frozen in that state and it's repulsive and frightening. It is also a lot of tension on your face. So start by relaxing your poor little face. What did it ever do to you? Give it a breather.

Sooner or later, you have to confront your anger in a healthy way where you won't feel stuck or powerless. Look at the real issue at hand rather than hiding behind the anger. Before you lose your temper or scream at someone, ask yourself these questions: "What/who is really making me angry? What is the real issue here? Can it hurt me or those I care about? Do I have the power to do something about it?" Yes, you do. You always do. This will also give you insight into your anger.

Release your anger in a positive way, in a positive place, where you don't have to fear any negative consequences. We've all had a few of those, we are sorry to say. A safe environment in therapy would be ideal, as well as a support group. One of my favorite ways to release anger when all else fails is to go to a quiet place, park my car there, roll up all the windows and then just scream and shout and let out everything that is pent up in me. It's invigorating. But make sure no one is around. Some people might get the wrong idea. Remember, you are not alone in being pissed off at any given time. Just don't let it take over and control you. Then, you've lost.

The good news is that anger slowly decreases with age, especially for those older than 50. I think one of the best things about being in midlife is that I simply don't have enough energy to be angry. I mean, it takes a lot of energy to be pissed off. And memory loss could sometimes be a good thing. By the time I come home, I've forgotten who I was mad at or what I was mad about. But I never forget what I want to eat and whom I want to cuddle with. Selective memory loss - now, that's brilliant!

There are many things in our lives we have no control over. But we do have control over how we will react and respond. We get to have the last word, whether we say it out or not. See, I told you there was something good about being middle-aged.

Have You Seen My Shrink?

*"After a year in therapy, my psychologist
said to me, 'maybe life isn't for everyone."*
Larry Brown

Psychotherapist:	*What brings you to therapy?*
Eunice:	*I have a decision to make.*
Psychotherapist:	*Okay.*
Eunice:	*It's my 45th birthday and I just need to decide whether I'll live or die today. That's all. You can help, right?*

I greatly admire people who go into psychotherapy, because it takes enormous courage to go into therapy, where one is willing to come face to face with one's painful and frightening issues, traumas, and skeletons in the closet, and confront them and demand resolution, truth, respect, honor, and mutual understanding. They are willing to journey into self-discovery. In return, they receive solace, enlightenment, and acceptance with oneself and others. *Wow!*

Not everybody can do this. As a matter of fact, most people will avoid their issues like the plague. But the ones who face them are the brave souls, who seek strength in themselves to have a better life, to be a better individual, and to have a greater, deeper human existence, AND not to drive their family members crazy.

No doubt, it's scary to face our demons, past and present. That's understandable. But the truth is, if you ignore your emotional issues, they rot in your body and mind, poisoning every aspect of your life. You can't run away from them, even though you may think you have it under control by keeping yourself busy or being in denial. They are alive inside of you, unresolved, and spreading like a disease. And all the self-defeating or self-medicating behavior won't make your emotional problems go away. It only leads to a further miserable existence, full of lies and deception to yourself and others you care about.

Luckily, you don't have to slay the emotional dragons alone. A competent and caring psychotherapist will help you process your issues one by one in a safe environment, so you can acknowledge, communicate, release, and even learn and grow from your psychological journey. Then, you can move on with your life, without the hidden chains and obstacles, which may be holding you back and even sabotaging your happiness, consciously or unconsciously. Psychotherapy can play a major role in the process of healing the mind and the soul.

Psychotherapist and clients are partners in one's self-discovery. In therapy, it's safe to be human. It's safe to be you without the necessary daily masks we wear to protect and shield ourselves from society. We can put aside our defense mechanisms for a while and just be. You can even vent a little, if you want.

There are many kinds of psychotherapy. Whether it's art or cognitive therapy or psychodrama, the goal is to face your issues, discover your true self, and draw strength and beauty from it, and move on and live.

It's a myth that psychotherapy is just for the mentally ill. On the contrary, it's for anyone interested in self-discovery. How can you deal with anything not knowing who you are and what you are made of, bad or good? It's the ultimate treasure hunt into yourself, body, mind, and soul.

People who go into therapy have the courage to ask for help. Not everybody can do this, either. Many stay wounded, proud, but ashamed their whole life. How sad and tragic, and they miss out on so much.

Be the one who journeys into oneself to break free from all the psychological obstacles that are holding you back. Isn't it time? And isn't discovering the treasures, strengths, and beauty in you worth a trip, an adventure? Remember, you don't have to do it alone. A professional and caring psychotherapist will be right beside you, cheering you on. *"You can do it! I got your back. We'll find the happiness in you together."*

Finding the Right Therapist

*"I told my therapist that everyone hates me.
He said I was being ridiculous –
everyone hasn't met me yet."*
Rodney Dangerfield

Finding the right psychotherapist is a lot like finding a soul mate. You need to invest a lot of time and energy, shop around, do your homework and legwork, be selective, and trust your gut.

A relationship with your therapist is going to be one of the most important relationships you'll have with another human being. Psychotherapy is a very personal experience where you are opening up and sharing some of your deepest, darkest, and most complex and traumatic times of your life, not to mention your hidden desires and secrets. You'll be vulnerable. You are letting someone see deep inside your heart, your psyche, and your soul. Therefore, it's crucial that you find someone you can trust thoroughly and completely all around.

The Three Cs a Therapist Must Have

Here are my criteria for what a psychotherapist must have based on my experience as a psychotherapist and a client.

Competency

Make sure your psychotherapist has the educational background and the clinical training, as well as the appropriate credentials. Ideally, a psychotherapist should have a master's degree or a doctorate in psychology or counseling, and be licensed or license-eligible. Ask about their background, education, experience, theoretical orientations, process, and fees. Interview them. This is going to be an important relationship, so ask lots of questions.

Caring

A psychotherapist should care about you genuinely and wholeheartedly with respect and understanding. I believe this is a field where one needs to be a good human being. If your therapist cares more about your money or your outfit, he or she is not the one for you.

A psychotherapist needs to really care about his or her clients and the profession. You just cannot fake it in this business. There's too much at stake. We are dealing with human lives and emotions here, not paperwork. So trust your instincts and make sure your psychotherapist is a good, kind, and caring individual.

Chemistry

Even if the psychotherapist has the perfect background and experience, but there's no chemistry between the two of you, he or she is not the right psychotherapist for you. There should be a rapport, a natural flow of communication, trust, understanding, compassion, and support. If a psychotherapist does not get you, and vice versa, it is not a good match.

You should feel totally comfortable with your psychotherapist with no reservations whatsoever. Ideally, a psychotherapist should be a total stranger who does not know anyone in your life, so he or she has no preconceived notions about you, and they can be completely objective about you and your issues. By the way, good psychotherapists should not have a lot of issues themselves, which could be dumped on the client unconsciously. If they have unresolved issues about gender, race, religion, or others, they cannot be objective. A good psychotherapist is always working on his or her own issues to make sure they remain objective, fair, and helpful to clients as much as possible.

This is very important: A psychotherapist should not be making decisions for you. If he or she is telling you what to do with your job, husband, wife, girlfriend, boyfriend, children, money, etc., this should be a warning sign in neon lights! Don't develop a dependency on your psychotherapist for answers and solutions. That is not their job. Unfortunately, there are unethical therapists who take advantage of their clients' desperation and vulnerability, physically, emotionally, and financially, so it's up to you to be aware and be in control. A psychotherapist should be helping you make your own decisions; otherwise you will always be dependent on him or her. A good psychotherapist should be a guide to help you see for yourself the causes of your unhappiness and the inner sources and solutions within you. So you can make your own decisions, and go on with your life, stronger, wiser, and proud to be in your skin.

Pay attention to all the feelings that arise during therapy and address them. Don't let them slide or sweep them under the rug. You're there to process your issues, not be polite.

It may take a while, but don't settle for a mediocre, second-rate psychotherapist. You cannot compromise yourself when it comes to your mind and soul.

Fun is Back Baby!

"Men and women do not quit playing because they grow old; they grow old because they quit playing."
Oliver Wendell Holmes

I never understood why life could not stay like kindergarten. We'd all go to work carrying a backpack and wearing our favorite flashing sneakers. We would work for awhile and then have recess, where we'd go outside and play and run around like mad, then come back inside and have a snack, work some more, take a nap, do finger painting, and then have lunch together sitting on a long bench. After lunch, we would work for a couple of hours, then go out for an afternoon recess, where we'd chase balls, jump rope, swing, and run around for no reason, other than it being ridiculously fun. Then, we'd take the bus home together, singing our favorite songs on the radio or making fun of the school bus driver's head. *Sorry.*

We'd come home, do some homework, eating milk and cookies. After that, we would go outside and run around with our friends and dogs, and then come inside and wash up for dinner. Imagine how much more productive and happier we grown-ups would be if there was recess in everybody's schedule at work. Recess should be mandatory in life.

Do you play in your life?

Do you remember how to play and what it is? By the time I was in midlife, I had completely forgotten what play was. I had to look it up and rediscover it. I've learned that it doesn't have to be elaborate; the simpler the better. For example, when was the last time you were on a swing? Yes, a swing. Go to a playground and get on a swing or go down on a slide. How about skipping? The second you start to skip, you just feel better all around and you start to giggle. You feel silly as can be, but it's so much fun, you can't stop. I bet it's been a lifetime since you've skipped. Go ahead, give it a go. Skip down the hallway, out the door, into the kitchen, to the copy room, bathroom, etc.

People will have that look that you're weird, but it's really envy, and besides, who cares?! You're having fun.

It's amazing how much fun these simple activities can be and it makes you smile, laugh, and be happy instantly. You feel like a kid again because you've never lost that. The poor child got shuffled temporarily as a grumpy grown-up, but the kid is back, *y'all!*

I love reading children's books once in awhile. It's simple, easy, and it has great pictures and even pop-ups. When life gets too complicated, I go to the children's section in a bookstore and read one of its books, and it puts things in perspective for me. It simplifies my day. I have something I understand and enjoy. I don't feel overwhelmed as a grown-up.

Don't ever stop being a kid. Bring out the child in you again, along with your childhood innocence, curiosity, eagerness, and enthusiasm. We need it more than ever. We may grow older physically, but the child inside us stays forever young. I think I'll be 10 today. That's when I was a munchkin in "The Wizard of Oz" play.

Put recess back into your life, where you go outside and play for just 10 to 15 minutes at least once a day. It will be good for your body, mind, and soul, and your co-workers, spouses, and kids will thank you, and join the fun. And stop growing up already. You've done enough of that. Put a playground in your office and put out some milk and cookies on your desk. It will do wonders, as it always has.

Daydream and Stay Sane in a Mad, Mad, Mad World!

"Everything you can imagine is real."
Pablo Picasso

Hi, my name is Clara and I am proud to say I suffer from the Walter Mitty Syndrome and I never want to be cured. Do you know about Walter Mitty? He is our kindred spirit and he lives inside every one of us.

Walter Mitty is a character played originally by the magnificent Danny Kaye in a movie titled, "The Secret Life of Walter Mitty," based on a book by James Thurber. In it, Mr. Mitty suffers from chronic daydreaming. Whether he's waiting for a traffic light to turn green or looking at a billboard, everything he sees he turns into a daydream, where he becomes a suave and irresistible hero who always saves a beautiful damsel in distress. Unfortunately, in real life, Mr. Mitty is a skinny, scrawny, petrified proofreader who gets bullied by his boss, coworkers, fiancée, mother, and Boris Karloff. *Yikes!*

I'm sure you've had a few daydreams yourself. I have. How can you not? It's the perfect temporary cure for real life. For me, it all began in school. During those long, boring, and confusing math classes, I would stare out the window, resting my cheek on my hands and just daydreaming away. Back then, I was obsessed with musicals and tap dancing, so I daydreamed about wearing stunning long gowns and dancing with Fred Astaire or Gene Kelly on stages, barnyards, ceilings, and in the glorious rain. Move over, Judy Garland! I was simply in heaven. I would have the longest stretch of grin on my face in my geometry class. And the best part was my teacher thought I was in love with math. Well, until I flunked the tests. I never got caught daydreaming. I was good at it. I would always sit at the desk in the back, right next to the window behind a very tall and wide student. It was the perfect place.

Real life, it's not so wonderful sometimes. So we create an imaginary world where we can have anything we want. Thank God for our imagination. It never grows old. If we only had reality, it would be the ultimate nightmare. I shiver just thinking about it.

Daydreaming is a way to escape when life becomes painful, boring, lonely, and unbearable at times. It's a temporary relief from being overwhelmed one way or another. It's a delightful pause in our often chaotic existence. And while we daydream, we heal a bit before returning to the reality we are bound to. So I daydream like Mr. Mitty once in awhile before going back to real life.

Escape into your own magical world, and remember, it's okay to be a hero or a damsel in distress, because in our daydreams, there are no rules. Anything goes. *How magical and wonderful!*

You're not in school any more, and you don't have to answer to parents or geometry teachers. You can daydream without being sent to the principal. Daydreaming is one of the greatest luxuries in life, and it's free. Just make sure you come out of it once in awhile, even though, at times, there may be no good reason to.

I keep one foot in the real world and the other foot in my imaginary world. I don't mind being "pixilated" once in a while. That's how I stay sane and happy in our *mad, mad, mad, mad world.*

We love you, Mr. Mitty.

Look for the Good in People, Not the Bad

*"If you look for the bad in people,
expecting to find it, you surely will."*
Abraham Lincoln

Sandra was born half Korean and half African-American. She never knew her real parents, as she was mysteriously dropped off at an orphanage during the Korean War. Nobody wanted her. The Americans said she wasn't American. The Koreans said she wasn't Korean. So she stayed in the orphanage where kids called her names for being racially mixed.

In the first few years of her life, Sandra was rarely touched, held, or loved. Then when she was 9 years old, a couple from the United States showed up and took her on an airplane for a very long ride. She didn't say a word. She just did what she was told to do by hand gestures. Sandra learned one thing: People were cold and mean. So that's all she expected.

I can relate to Sandra. When I was in the 5th grade, we had to write that universal essay on "What I want to be when I grow up." While I was imagining being all kinds of things, like a ballerina or an astronaut, my teacher came up to me and said, "You don't have to think about it, dear. You'll probably be a maid or work in a grocery store." I kid you not. A "teacher" told a young, vulnerable child, a student of hers that she can never dream. I was told I had no right because I was not White. The teacher would repeat this over and over until I graduated, so I wouldn't forget. And I didn't. How could I?

My first love was ballet and I danced almost every chance I got. When I was 12 years old, there was an opening for a ballet scholarship. But my dance teacher told me, "You can't be a ballerina. No one will pay money to see a yellow swan!"

When I was working in TV, I pitched a talk show to a program executive and he said, "No American will listen to an Oriental talk for more than 10 seconds, so forget about it. It will never ever happen." Gee, I wonder why I became so jaded. *Hmmm.* I spent a lot of my life sobbing silently in the bathroom stalls.

Based on my life experience, I was convinced that most people were mean and horrible. When I saw someone walking toward me, I put up my guard and my mental dukes. I believed that somehow they were going to hurt me. That's how I went through life, surrounding myself with all the guards and defense mechanisms I could muster. That's how it was for a long time.

Then one day, someone blew me away by being good and kind. I went into shock. I froze for awhile. What is this? This person was good to me for no reason. No reason! I was highly suspicious at first. But she didn't want anything from me. She was just "good." She said,

"Look for the good in people and you'll find it. Look for the bad in people and you'll find that, too. The world is full of good people. They're a little harder to find because they don't seek the spotlight. They are not loud but quiet and humble. There are people who roam this planet doing good for no reason at all. And, dear Clara, you are one of them."

Either she was completely crazy or she was right.

I set out to do a scientific experiment. I went out on the street and deliberately focused on seeing only the good in each person I encountered. Whether it was a teacher, a lawyer, a mailman, a cashier at the grocery store, or a vice president of a corporation, I looked for the good in them. Then I wrote it all down and kept a record of it. I even approached the "bad people" I had horrible experiences with and looked for the good in them. I really didn't want to, but I forced myself in the name of science. It required a lot of digging, patience, and extended compassion, but I did it. In some people, good was quite difficult to find, but in the end, I've discovered there's at least one good thing in most people. When I was good to others, the response was usually positive. It's hard to be mean to someone who is so nice to you. So I decided to focus on the good side of people. And, wouldn't you know it? I felt lighter, happier, and slept better at nights. My guards took a much needed break and my mental boxing gloves were put on the shelves, at least for now.

The Dalai Lama said most people are a combination of some good and bad. I think he's right. So I made a choice. I will consciously look for the good in people and connect and build on that. It's definitely more pleasant. Besides, I've already seen the bad side and I don't need to see more of that, over and over. I've also learned to look for good in myself as well. Nobody ever tells us this. But it's true. There's so much good in you. I mean, TONS! And midlife is saying, "Come on out already!" We've already had all sorts of life experiences, and we are still here, standing.

It turned out that Sandra's adopted parents were very kind and loving. At first, Sandra rejected their affection, not understanding what it was. She didn't even know what a hug was. But the parents persevered with patience and unfailing devotion, and as time passed, Sandra gave into their tender, loving care, soaking it all in as she was starved of all that was good. And in return, Sandra became a good, kind, and loving person herself. Sandra grew up and became an engineer. She married her college sweetheart and decided to adopt three children from orphanages in the U.S. and around the world. How powerful a little good can be.

By the way, I think people who adopt children are angels and heroes. They are extraordinary ordinary people, and I admire them greatly. My two cents worth. Thank you.

What Is This Thing Called Loneliness?

*"The worst loneliness is
not to be comfortable with yourself."*
Mark Twain

A Letter from Isabel:

"I knew it was coming.
The evening started out like any other night. I had a light dinner, cleaned up, and took care of some chores and paid the necessary bills and put them in the mailbox with the red flag up.

It was finally time to rest and wind down for the night. Without a minute to breathe, the night stalker began its unwelcome entrance. I felt its dark presence from a distance. The cold, damp, and thorny hands were reaching for my soul. I didn't have a chance. I was thoroughly alone.

My usual defenses against loneliness were futile, but I headed to the kitchen anyway for all that my tummy could consume. I turned on the TV to hear another person's voice. I made calls only to get artificial greetings, and the work I tried to do so dutifully rejected me. Nothing could comfort the howling, empty night, where the pangs of my loneliness screamed endlessly, suffocating me ever so slowly. The night never seemed to end. All kinds of time stopped. Even after all the food, the liquor, and the endless B movies on TV, I could still feel the cold wet hands of loneliness. I could not fight it. It was inside my whole being now. Finally, I surrendered and fell into a subconscious coma, where nightmares danced inside of me until the sun came up."

In the morning, they found Isabel unconscious with barely a pulse. A neighbor noticed her cat scratching at the door. She had overdosed on all the pills in her medicine cabinet. She had done this before.

Isabel was beautiful, smart, and kind. They all asked why she would do this to herself? What could be missing in her life, to be so miserable, so frightened, and so sad? No one knew, except for Isabel, who could not escape the curse of loneliness.

What is this thing called loneliness?
Everybody has experienced it to some degree. It can be unbearable and maddening.

It turns out that loneliness is not about the absence of another person physically, but the absence of a genuine emotional connection. You could be lonelier when you're with the wrong person or in a crowded room. I'm sure you've experienced this first hand. Perhaps, you are lonely for yourself. The person who is missing in your life could be you.

Loneliness can be very distressing, painful, dehumanizing, self-defeating, empty, and full of unbearable sadness. It's also been linked to health issues such as depression, anxiety, addiction, alcoholism, physiological problems, and suicide. Some people even spend time with destructive people, believing that being with anyone, even bad and negative people is better than being alone. But it often backfires.

Sadly, loneliness can also kill. I've seen unfortunate souls who have taken their own lives, unable to bear the invisible, silent pain in their hearts and souls. People resort to all kinds of desperate self-destructive behavior to drown and mask their agonizing loneliness, which only leads to further isolation and even poor health. According to a study from Brigham Young University, loneliness is worse for your overall health than smoking 15 cigarettes a day.

Yet another study came out recently that showed, despite the internet connection and each of us carrying a cell phone, we are more isolated, lonely, and disconnected. It has lead to depression, rage, and self-defeating behavior. I wish we could all just sit down at a big table and just eat and talk together without phones, laptops, or iPods. We've been doing it for centuries, and now we've lost our most precious human connection to survive and to love.

We've all been burned, betrayed, and hurt by people, big time. We have good reasons to be weary, guarded, and cautious, so we naturally put up defense mechanisms to protect ourselves and our vulnerable hearts. I totally understand. But it can also work against us as well. The longer our guards are up, the longer and more deeply we'll be lonely.

One of the greatest fears in life is growing old alone, that no one will be around to care for us when we are physically unable to. According to a study by Moustakes, the fear of getting old alone far outweighs the fear of death. It's true. We are not islands. We cannot survive on our own, especially emotionally. We need a genuine and loving human connection, where we give, receive, nurture, love, and are loved for our entire lifetime.

While immersed in my neurotic midlife crisis, I've decided to take charge of my own loneliness. I've seen too many folks in hospitals, clinics, and convalescent homes withering away alone, and I didn't want to end up like them. So, I developed a daily/monthly/yearly plan to avoid being lonely. First, I acknowledged the fact that if I wanted a genuine emotional connection, I also had to offer it. It can't be a one-way deal.

I also noticed that active and outgoing people were far less lonely. That makes sense. The worst thing you can do when you're lonely is to be alone. I created a list of five people I can call, five things I can do, and five places I can go to alleviate my loneliness. Just having the list made me less lonely and vulnerable. I also faced my biggest obstacle: ME, MYSELF, AND I! I needed to get out of my own way. I was legitimately scared. Unbeknownst to me, I had created a pretty solid wall around me. No one could penetrate it. I'm not the only one. Many people built walls around to keep pain and rejection out. The problem with walls is that nothing good can come in, either, and we can't be happy alone in a mental fortress. So I confronted my issues and forged ahead with my eyes open. It was scary to let down my guard down once in awhile, but it was time to open up my heart again and let it do its job: *Love.* Besides, I didn't want the alternative.

By the way, there is a difference between loneliness and being alone. I've learned to be comfortable being alone, enjoying my own company; the joy of one. You can't always be with someone. So take in the beauty of all that is you and your surroundings and let it soothe you. People who are able to enjoy being alone are more secure with themselves and the world. They are not dependent or desperate as much. So when loneliness comes around, you won't be emotionally devastated. You won't be frightened or self-destructive, either.

Loneliness is another state of being. As long as it's not excessive or debilitating, it's not a threat. As a matter of fact, a little down time alone can be relaxing, calming, and healing. Know that it's normal and natural to feel lonely from time to time. It's not a personality or character flaw. You don't have to be with someone every second of the day. How exhausting that would be.

However, I don't have to be entirely alone. I never get tired of the company of my wonderful, loyal, fuzzy four-legged friends. They have soothed my loneliness and life's other painful moments with unconditional love, loyalty, understanding, quirkiness, and joy for a long time. So I guess I was really never alone.

Make sure you surround yourself with people of quality. Nothing feels emptier and lonelier than being with a bunch of people who are artificial, unkind, and demeaning. Forget the flakes. We've all had enough of them. Be with real people who are not full of themselves.

The good thing is that you have the power to minimize your own loneliness. If you fear being alone, do something about it NOW. No one else can do this for you. You have to reach out to people and work on building healthy, deep, genuine, and sincere relationships. It cannot be selfish or superficial. Create the possibilities not to be lonely.

Remember, take action and reach out. Also, learn to enjoy your own company. Put your guard down from time to time, or at least build an entrance door. Choose real people over fakes, and keep an open mind.

Have you heard of the buddy bench?
Kids from Willowgrove School in Saskatoon, a city in Saskatchewan, Canada, designed it for lonely kids during recess, who didn't have anyone to play with, as well as had a hard time asking a group if they could join in. We've all been there. The bench has also become an anti-bullying method. It has become highly successful.

Boy, do grown-ups need a buddy bench, too. It can be like pulling teeth to get two strangers to say a few words to each other without passing out from anxiety. Just because we are big now doesn't mean talking to others or asking if they want to hang out is any easier. It might even be tougher than when we were kids. So, if all else fails, let's get a buddy bench for grown-ups.

I loved this idea so much, I tried it myself and it was magical. It became a neutral and natural way to make new pals without all the formalities. Give it a try. Put a buddy bench at your work, house, playground, or wherever you think buddies can be born, and watch loneliness melt away.

If You Wanna Be Happy for the Rest of Your Life, *EXERCISE!!!*

"God gave you only one body,
so you better be nice to it.
Exercise, because if you don't,
by the time you're our age,
you'll be pushing up daisies."
Sadie Delaney, 102

We can hardly keep up with all the reports and studies that prove exercise can prevent, alleviate and even cure just about any and all illnesses, physical and mental. Exercise helps our bodies to get in shape, to stay young, to function longer and better, to prevent heart disease to cancer, to lose weight, to keep the circulation flowing in the brain (as well as the mind), to lift depression, and even to increase self-esteem, just to mention a few. I've also heard plastic surgeons swear that exercising can defy and reverse aging. So, if you're looking for a magic pill, EXERCISE is it!

The thing is our bodies were designed to move throughout our lives. We cannot sit still for a long time. It's quite bad for us in every way. Now, we all know that exercise is good for us, and yet most people will not do it. Why? Why won't people exercise when they know it can help them become healthy, lose weight, look younger, and even save their lives? Well, it's not the exercise that's the problem. It's the image associated with exercise that causes most people to run for a doughnut. I had the same problem. I put on my workout outfit and just stared at the treadmill. It's now become a clothes rack.

Most people associate exercise with pain. It's hard, unpleasant, boring, messy, and time-consuming. It may bring up issues we don't want to look at, such as being overweight, unhealthy, lazy, inflexible, and being plain scared. For most of us, the bottom line is: Exercise is just no fun in any way. We get as far as buying all the right exercise outfits, gear, equipment, and a membership to the gym, but that's when it all stops. It's back to the couch with potato chips and ice cream. So I came up with a treatment that worked for both myself and my patients. I associated exercise with pleasure and fun, and it worked. We all lost weight, became healthier, felt younger and better all around, and left therapy. *Woohoo!*

When we think of exercise, most of us think about Nautilus equipment, running for miles huffing and puffing, lifting weights, jumping up and down for an hour, and trying to touch your toes in agonizing pain. It's really, really hard, and who wants to be seen wearing those tight clothes bouncing all over the place? It may be for some people, but not for everybody, especially those over 40. But exercise doesn't have to come only in the form of heavy equipment or intense sweating. As a matter of fact, moderate exercise has a higher success rate than any radical or heavy-duty workout. After all, our ancestors exercised without any weights, gyms, and treadmills and they were thinner and healthier.

The key is to find a form of exercise you actually enjoy doing. Some examples are dancing, sports, and walking with buddies. By the way, walking is one of the greatest forms of exercise around. Most people can do it, and you learned it early in life. Just put one foot in front of the other and go. Walking is also less likely to cause injuries, because you're not pouncing on your ankles or knees. You're also putting fresh air into your lungs. Plus, you can walk longer than you can run. It's even better if you walk with your dogs. You'll both get great exercise, keep each other company, meet people and pooches on the street, and have loads of fun.

There are also people walking in groups all over the place, including cities, parks, stairs, malls, mountains, rooftops, etc. They meet on a regular basis and just walk together, talking, laughing and sharing. They're not just building their muscles, but friendships and communities, which are known to increase longevity and health, among other things. Exercise and social connection: *Brilliant combination.*

My exercise thing is dancing. I love to dance. It's endless fun and I can't get enough of it. I get to hear great music, meet and dance with people, sweat and burn calories, and learn a new step every time. It's a win-win. And the best thing about dancing is that I don't look at it as exercise. It's simply fun and it's good for my body and my mind, not to mention my social life. The endorphins are multiplying like mad. And, by the way, some of the longest-lived and healthiest people around don't even have an exercise plan. They just move most of the day working in the field, gardening, cooking, etc. They are moving constantly. That's the key.

Everybody has an activity they enjoy, whether it's playing tag, football, ice skating, doing the cha cha, tap dancing, ice hockey, the hustle, or just shaking the bootie with the music blasting in your room. Remember, exercise has to be FUN. It has to be associated with pleasure rather than pain. When you're exercising for fun, you won't even know that your heart is getting stronger or that you're building muscles, lowering your cholesterol, lifting your depression, reducing the risk of high blood pressure, stroke, and heart disease, strengthening mobility and balance, getting those buns of steel, increasing your vitality and lifespan, making your bones stronger, losing weight, slowing down memory loss, building your immune system, reducing the risk for Alzheimers and keeping bowels regular (hey, this is important stuff!), and so much more. There isn't a single thing where exercise can't help. You'll also make new friends and have the time of your life.

Exercise is also great to melt stress away. Not to mention, the more you exercise, the more you get to eat! That is the best incentive for me. So go for it. Dig out those good ol' 45s, albums, and CDs from the garage and blast the music and dance the night away; call a friend and go boogie; pick up that tennis racket in the back of the closet and go hit a few balls; sign up for a basketball team, yoga, or swing class. By the way, ballroom dancing has returned with a vengeance. Remember, go and move and have FUN!

Gotta Dance!

Independence
It Ain't for Sissies!

*"You are all you've got.
Don't compromise yourself."*
Katherine Hepburn

Independence is one of the most important assets for both women and men at any age, but it's especially crucial in the second half of our lives. The last thing we want is to be dependent on someone when we are older. *No thanks!* So get yourself together. As Bette Davis said, *"Old age ain't no place for sissies!"*

Independence gives you physical, financial, and emotional freedom to own your life and to be your own self. It gives you choices to live your life the way you want to, be with whoever you want to, and create and direct your own destiny. With independence, you are in control of your life.

Being independent also gives you self-confidence, which will help you make positive choices in your life and pursue healthier relationships. Being dependent on anyone creates self-defeating behaviors and desperate situations. It can also be dangerous, because no one can be with you forever, even if they want to. The last thing you want is to be a burden on anyone in your later years, especially your children.

Being dependent can also perpetuate low self-esteem, which could lead to all kinds of life's little traps. You should be the main person you lean on. You are the only person who will be with you until the very end. So work on YOU all the time. This should be one of your top priorities.

I was dating a guy right out of college. I was in between jobs and unsure about what to do with my life. Without even knowing it, I made my boyfriend my life. I doted on him, cooked for him, waited for him, shopped for him...*you know where I'm going with this.* Anyway, my boyfriend became very unhappy and upset. The more I did wonderful things for him 24/7, the more he wanted to get away from me. He finally said he didn't want to be my whole life. He ended up resenting me. Then, he took up with another woman, an independent woman, who had a profession, a social life, her own place, who barely gave him the time of day, let alone iron his clothes, clean his bathroom, and shine his shoes. What up?!

Don't make my mistake.
Make independence the foundation of your life. From there, you can build your life, your own home, and your own dreams. Independence is also a necessary survival tool and a great gift to give to yourself and to those you love and cherish.

To achieve independence, you have to acquire the basic human needs, such as food, clothing, and shelter. So get an education and/or develop a skill to make yourself marketable, so you can be employed by others or yourself, which will (hopefully) produce an income to live on. Then you can get your own home, buy food, a car, and clothing, and have the freedom to pursue your dreams, and help your family and friends.

An education is one of the basic and necessary components in developing independence that helps you become a decision maker in all aspects of your life. Knowledge really does give you power. It also opens your mind to new possibilities, expands your horizon, and gives you unlimited choices. And the best part is you're never too young or old to learn anything.

As a matter of fact, studies show learning something new and challenging keeps our brain cells multiplying and thus keeps the mind sharp. It can slow down memory loss, prevent dementia, Alzheimer's, among other things. The brain will literally deteriorate without any intellectual stimulus. So, feed it some brain food and let it work for you. Don't be idle with your brain. It is a muscle, so use it or lose it. Whether it's getting a degree, playing a video game or chess, or trying a new set of recipes, keep learning, no matter what.

Today, we have more choices for education than ever, and going back to school is not the only option for educating ourselves. It's literally at our fingertips. The Internet is a great and free source for information and education. Just make sure you visit legitimate sources. If you don't have a computer, go to your library, where information, assistance, and knowledge await you, and it's all free.

Read whenever possible. I mean real stuff and not just your emails and texts. Start by reading books, especially classical ones, and don't be afraid to ask a lot of questions. You can also take night classes, study by correspondence, take online courses, or even audit a course in college. Information is available everywhere. Studies have shown that children and adults who are avid readers fare better in life in terms of livelihood and self-esteem. Reading also helps us soar with imagination, takes us on exciting adventures and romances, and lets us be whomever we want to be, from a princess to a scientist.

Good or bad, money is reality. It *does* make the world go around.

Often times, women are discouraged from knowing about money. Their fathers or their husbands or even their sons take care of the finances in the household, leaving women uninformed about their own financial situations. Money is considered dirty and complicated for women to understand. *Well, it's time to get your hands dirty, ladies!*

Whether you're single or married, young or old, man or a woman, everyone should know how to make money, how to invest and save money, and how to make it work for them for the rest of their lives. You should always be informed and in control over your financial situation. And it's not hard. All it takes is a little knowledge and planning. Don't leave money matters to others. This is your responsibility and you cannot blame anyone but yourself. You need to be in charge of your own finances and know where every dollar goes or stays.

In order to have total independence, you need some money to back it up. Without financial security, you will always be dependent on someone, and you can't have complete independence when you are relying on others for money. I can't emphasize enough the importance and the necessity for financial security, which gives you independence and freedom to pursue personal interests, travel, make charitable contributions, and make a difference in your own lives, as well as others.

Earning your money also gives you self-worth. You are being rewarded for your contribution and talents, and for making a difference in our society. All this creates a higher sense of self-esteem. You start to feel good about yourself, and that in return will reflect on everything you do and in all your relationships.

It is also important how you make your money. You need to have faith in your work and in yourself. It's very gratifying to earn your own living making a difference and/or doing what you enjoy. If you are making money illegally or doing something you loathe or that makes you feel that you're selling out, you are robbing yourself of peace of mind, self-respect, and dignity. Don't sell your soul for cash. You will begin to hate and lose yourself and create a separate hell for yourself, and happiness will be lost.

We spend most of our lives working. So make sure it's something you enjoy and are proud of doing, where you can learn, grow, enjoy, contribute, and hopefully help someone other than yourself. All this will lead to INDEPENDENCE!

I'm sure you've heard that the secret to making money is doing something you love. When you do something you love, the money will follow. The other way rarely works. Also, make sure you don't become a slave to money, like so many people. Nothing could be more miserable and sad. Also, debt can be a scary thing. People have killed themselves over it. Money isn't everything. It's only an avenue to cover our basic needs and to provide reasonable comfort.

There's a trend of people downsizing and even moving into tiny homes to reduce being a slave to debt and material things. They also eliminated credit cards. So far, they seem to be content with more time for family and friends, peace of mind, and to really enjoy their one and only life in the present moment without worrying so much about money.

What about the idea of "living within our means?" I have a friend who is a single parent with two teenage kids. She earns more than $10,000 a month, but feels it's not nearly enough. I asked her what amount would be enough. She didn't know, but it would have to be "way more." Then, she shooed me away because she had to work to make more money. She does the same to her kids. Then, I suggested the notion of trying to live within the means of $10,000 dollars a month income, (that's $120,000/yr) rather than frantically trying to make more money all the time and stressing out about it. According to the U.S. Census, the median household income for 2014 was $52,789. Only about 20% of Americans break the six figure annually.

I try to live within my means now. I can't tell you how much stress melted away. I am fairly content with what I have. And unless it's absolutely necessary, I try not to buy it, because I already have enough things in my house, big or small that I don't need or will ever use taking up valuable space. I also like to give things away rather than acquire things. You can donate and help someone in need rather than things just wasting away in your basement. Also, why not improve on the items you have, like furniture, rather than buying new ones, that cost more money and space? No doubt, there are a lot of mini hoarders out there.

Money doesn't equate to happiness. Studies show consistently that having a lot of money does not buy happiness. As a matter of fact, there was no difference in the happiness level of someone with a $5000 a month and $50,000 a month income. You will have to determine how much money will make you comfortable. You may be surprised how little that could be.

By all means, make the effort to make, save and build for the future, but don't become a slave to money and income. It can be a bottomless pit and you might fall in. *Ouch!*

Positive Calls Only...*Please*

"I'm only home to happy people."
Unknown

I only take positive calls now.

It doesn't matter whether it's family members, total strangers, or those annoying and rude sales people who call during dinner time, I only take positive calls, period. This is another survival tactic of mine. It's a matter of life and death in many ways, because negative people can kill and it's often a slow, tortuous, agonizing death. *You know what I mean.* And I've had enough of that. A lifetime's worth.

For my entire life, I took calls from everybody.

Everyone called to complain, whine, moan and groan, sob, and then complain, whine, and moan and sob again, on and on, for hours, from different times and places on earth. I didn't know it at the time, but all that negative and toxic dumping on me affected my psyche and made me jaded beyond words. It also turned me into a whiner as well, as I got caught up in all the negative talk and attitude. Afterwards, I had a headache and wanted to jump off a bridge, and I wasn't even having a bad day. I also felt de-energized, depressed, and exhausted. This was not healthy.

The minute people found out I was a psychologist, I became a sitting duck. They just assumed I wanted to hear their problems and their uninteresting secrets and desires. It was a hostage situation and I was too polite and stupid to cut them off and walk away. So, I came home carrying more garbage on my poor psyche. They sucked the life out of me and I had none to give to those whom I cared about.

After the cancer treatment, I could no longer be a dumping ground. I had to survive and take care of myself first. No more door mat or tire marks on my face or anywhere else. So, no more negative calls. No exceptions! Period. I made an announcement to my family and friends: "*Only positive calls from now on. Thank you.*" If they had a problem or needed to vent, I was more than happy to refer them to a psychotherapist, a pastor, or a statue. I was a bit flexible with family members. For example, when my sister called to whine about her two teenagers, I would give her exactly 5 minutes to vent and then I would give her my positive input for a minute and then only positive talk, otherwise sayonara!

I also grew distant from constantly negative people in my life. I'm sure you have a few. These are people who made a lifetime career of complaining, criticizing, bitching, and being negative. Nothing is ever good or right. They seem to relish and enjoy it. Why were they in my life? The problem is they'll drag you down with them and before you know it, you've become a negative and toxic person yourself.

For negative people with whom I wanted to continue a relationship or a friendship, I sat them down and had an honest talk. Most people don't even know they are being negative. And honestly, you could be helping them snap out of that horrible habit. So it would help everybody.

It may sound harsh, but this is absolutely crucial to my survival now; to anybody's survival. I cannot be healthy or happy with negative and toxic people polluting my body and mind, destroying all that is positive, hopeful, and good. Atomic bombs, pollution, pesticide, and radiation are not the only toxic things out there. People are on the top of the list. So stay away from negative people and take only positive calls. It will do wonders and make you happy.

What My Fortunetellers Taught Me

"I don't believe in fortunetellers.
I just go to one."
Dr. Clara

When I was able to walk, my mother took me to see a fortuneteller, as Asian folks often do. There, a shaman-like lady wearing a long silky yellowish-red robe summoned me into an incense-filled gray room. After a short ritual of some kind, lots of writing and chanting, she told my mother I would not have such a great life. She shook her head back and forth saying I had a "tough fate that cannot be bent." Then, she walked away, still shaking her bald head. My mother left an "offering" on a gold tray.

When I graduated from college, my mom took me to see a fortuneteller, as Asian folks often do when a daughter reaches a certain age. It was mainly to see when I would get married and if we could speed up the process. He said he couldn't see "marriage or a husband," in my fate. Instead, he said, I would be in education. "What a dope!" I'd thought. Is he crazy?! I hated school and studying. And besides, I was planning on being a wife and mother by the time I was a cool 25 years of age. Thank you very much!

When I was in my 30s, I went to go see a fortuneteller, as Asian women often do when they're not getting married and having kids. The fortuneteller touched my face, grabbed my hands, scribbled Chinese characters and numbers on a notepad and said, "You are suffering from depression. You are seriously depressed!" I said, "Thank you?" handing him 50 dollars. When I got home, I realized I was wearing someone else's shoes.
(It's customary to take your shoes off in Asian homes, Buddhist temples, and fortunetellers' homes.)

When I was in midlife, I went to go see a fortuneteller, as Asian folks often do when their life seems stuck and unhappy. A Buddhist monk calmly flipped through an old worn out tablet full of beautiful Chinese characters. Then he wrote down my birthday, the time I was born, and then he told me that "it would be difficult."

"What? My life?" I said, talking back to a fortuneteller for the first time in my whole life. I asked him to elaborate, *please*....

"Clouds," he said.

"Clouds? Can you be more specific?" I said, apologizing for talking back.

"Whatever in your life, it's like trying to catch a cloud in your hand. Nothing solid can come of it, let alone catch anything that can be yours." Giving out a deep, long, slow, and loud sigh while shaking his head, he said, "Your fate in life is a lonely one. No man. No children. No money. No house. No, *well*..." He stopped for awhile to clean his pristine glasses.

After another slow, agonizing sigh, he continued, "I'm afraid you have a sad weeping ghost living in your soul. You have bad karma."

"A sad weeping ghost?" I said quietly. What the heck is that? I froze with my mouth wide open. I stopped blinking. I thanked him and carried my shoes home.

After my cancer treatment, I went to see a fortuneteller, as Asian folks often do when they feel scared and lost, and can't find anything else to hold onto. The monk took a long, deep look at my face and said, "You have a sad life....*A very sad life*." At that moment, without holding myself back like a good Asian girl, I burst into tears and started sobbing with both my hands over my face. All went silent in the temple.

I wasn't sure if I should think about my sad life or why I keep going to see fortunetellers. I spiraled down into a deep despair and wondered if I should stay alive. The fortuneteller was right about one thing: I was seriously depressed, more than he could ever imagine.

So, what now? I'd thought. What exactly am I supposed to do with a sad, lonely, difficult life with no man, children, money, or home, and with depression, cancer, AND clouds that can't be caught, not to mention a weeping ghost in my soul, who won't go away? Jumping off the cliff was the first thing that came to my mind. But then, I got hungry.

The problem is that anyone could be a "fortuneteller." The hardest part is finding one who is somewhat legit. That's why I prefer

Buddhist monks; not so much to get fortunetelling, but to gain some
inkling of wisdom, peace, and compassion. Plus, they always offer you
free meals made of wonderful mountain vegetables and great tea,
and they are kind and calm. I love Buddhist temples. I find them so
tranquil, beautiful, and spiritual, and everybody leaves me alone.

A few years ago, I came upon a female monk after my breast
cancer treatment. She was young, just 40 and attractive, even with no
make-up and a shaved head. She was warm, kind, and very open. I
haven't known someone like that most of my life. She said little, but
was very attentive and listened whole-heartedly, without glancing at
the clock. I haven't experienced something like that much either. It
was both surreal and soothing. She didn't tell my fortune, but she told
me that I am probably more courageous than I know. Then, she gave
me a book, her one and only copy.

That reminded me of the few kind remarks I received in the
past. One was by a woman who rescued horses. As I was getting in
my car, she yelled out, "Clara, you have so much to give. I'm not sure
if you know that." I waved goodbye awkwardly, drove down the hill,
pulled over, and sobbed.

The other was a ballet teacher, who told me I was a beautiful
ballet dancer with beauty and grace, and I should not forget it, even
in midlife. I was shocked. I had to leave the room. I went into the
bathroom and sobbed. A few genuine, kind, and warm words from
strangers and the world looked like a decent place and I could fly like
Superman.

I no longer go to fortunetellers.
I'm not sure if my life was sad because they said it would be, or
because it was my destiny. Who knows? I don't care anymore. I'm old
enough where my energy and time are precious and I don't waste
them on things that have no answers or make no sense.

I focus on the present now. It's all I have. All I know. I focus on
the positive and take one footstep at a time in life and just keep
moving with a smile on my face. From time to time, there are
teardrops along the way, as it is part of anyone's life, but eventually,
the sun comes back out and I see hummingbirds and bees buzzing
around, busy at work, and I look up at the blue sky, where there are

always some fluffy white clouds I can never hold in my hands. So I lie on the ground and turn them into cute giant animals, and that makes me happy. I like elephants the best. And the weeping ghost is still with me, still weeping away, sometimes bellowing out of control. So be it. I'm gonna go eat.

The Dream That Saved My Life

"I dream. Sometimes I think that's the only right thing to do."
Haruki Murakami

My first dream in life was an unoriginal one. With many little girls in the universe, I wanted to be a ballerina. So, when we immigrated to America, my mom took me to ballet classes. Proudly, I had my pink tights, pink ballet shoes, pink ballet bag, and pink hair ribbon in my hair. I was in. I was even given a semi-important role as a munchkin in *The Wizard of Oz*. I couldn't be considered for any leading roles, which were reserved for little White girls.

I truly loved ballet. It felt so natural to me and I was happy when I was dancing. And, dare I say it? I was pretty good at it. Unfortunately, my parents couldn't afford the classes and I had to stop for awhile. I picked it up again later in life when I started making my own money. But life got in the way, as it has a tendency to do: college, finances, work, bills, disappointments, and a broken heart.

When I was in college, I used to ditch classes and head to my ballet classes instead. Of course, my grades suffered and my advisor told me I was the only Asian student with a "C" average in math and science classes. Apparently, I was a "Bad Asian." I was warned, but it hardly shook me. I used to take as many as five ballet classes a week. I didn't mind the aches and pain and the inevitable blisters and sore muscles. It was all heavenly to me. It's funny how you don't feel any pain when you're doing something you love. It was like riding on a cloud. It was easy, beautiful, and glorious. As I grew older, life became more serious and I couldn't find the time to continue ballet. So, I buried my pink ballet leotards, tights, and shoes in the closet and went on with reality.

I'm not sure why exercising becomes harder as you grow older. Is it time, aging body, or all of the above? But it became almost impossible to get to it. Although I walked my dogs every day, I was told that wasn't enough -- not when I was fighting cancer. So exercise had to come front and center.

I'm not what you call an athletic type. I'm not a gym person either. So there was only one option: Dance. Ballet. It was serious exercise and I enjoyed it, which meant I would most likely stick to it. However, I was much older now and my body was stiffer than last year's fruit cake in the freezer, and my ballet stuff was buried somewhere where things cannot be found or returned.

It must have been at least 15 years since my last ballet class. That's a millennium in ballet time. It took me months to get the courage to actually take a class. I was older, weaker, and just plain terrified. But one miraculous day, when it was pouring rain, I dug through my closet for hours and got my ancient ballet stuff out and drove myself to class and didn't look back.

With a sagging leotard, not to mention body parts, faded pink tights a size or two too small now, outdated ballet shoes that reeked of moth balls, I walked cautiously into a class. I'd thought I would be the oldest student in an intermediate class. After all, I was in my 50's. But it turned out that the two of the best students were 80 and 84 years young. Imagine that! And the teacher wasn't a large frightening woman, ready to tell me there was still no such thing as a "yellow swan." As a matter of fact, the teacher complimented me and said I was a beautiful dancer on my first day. He doesn't know it. But I cried the whole way home. What a pleasant surprise! I never expected that. So my ballet journey was reborn and I'm still on it.

Honestly, ballet is hard and my body takes a beating. It takes discipline, coordination, concentration, and grace while twisting, turning, jumping, and leaping everywhere to beautiful and timeless classical music. But it's pure happiness. If I'm lucky, I'll be dancing ballet well into my 80s like my co-swans in ballet heaven. Thank you, dear old dream, for coming to my rescue. You saved my body, life, and soul. *Now, point your toes!*

You Are Enough Now

"Happiness can only exist in acceptance."
George Orwell

What an unbelievable notion.
If I didn't hear it from someone else, it would've never occurred to me on my own. Even if it did, I would not have believed it.
Not too long ago, I heard someone say, "Why can't you be enough the way you are right now? Why do you need to be more?' I froze from confusion and shock. Nothing on me moved. "What?" was my only response.

Only human beings judge each other by status, looks, race, weight, age, and on and on. I mean, what is the first thing we say to each other when we met? "So, what do you do?" "Well, I read, I cook, I walk, I sing and I do a mean cha cha." How's that for an answer?!

We are conditioned to constantly go after things, and then more things. We are told to keep climbing the work ladder, accumulate as many things as possible (it's like a race), reach for VIP status every single stinking minute. If your neighbor has a Mercedes, you have to have one, too. Why? Why can't you and I be enough the way we are now, with or without titles, money, a college degree or hair? I couldn't find a good answer.

Why can't we be enough the way we are? Why can't we just be? I had to see this for myself. So, I set aside a whole day where I did not try to get everything done, get to the next level in work and life, be everything to everyone, but just be. Eat. Walk. Read. Look out the window. Chat with my neighbors. Help out a friend with no pre-planned agenda or an organized schedule of any kind. *Whoa!* It was surreal. I felt I was living. I felt free.

It doesn't mean you have to stop improving on yourself. It's not about that at all. By all means, we were designed for progress, so we will always evolve and move forward, but it doesn't have to take over our whole life, every day. Would it matter so much if we didn't get the master's degree, move to a bigger house, buy a better car, have the latest phone, have less wrinkles, or wear a trendy outfit? Who is telling us that it's not good enough, and why the heck do we care? They are likely strangers or folks that don't know or care about us. So why bother?

I've been a victim of prejudice of all kinds in my life and it still continues. I've been discriminated against because of my gender, height, race, age, not having status, not having money, for having dogs, and even having cancer, just to mention a few. Seriously, why do we put up with this?

I took a bold step and decided that I am enough the way I am now, warts and all. I will continue to learn, improve myself, work to make a difference, and search for even a better chocolate cake, but I have decided that I am enough the way I am. Even if I never "improve," I am okay. It won't mean I am any less of a human being. Besides, I should be the only one to be a judge of that.

As far as all the stuff we acquire and chase after, when it's time for us to go, we cannot take a single thing with us, not even my teeth.

So remember, you are good enough the way you are right now, period.

Conclusion

Life still doesn't make a whole lot of sense to me. Even as I grow older, that remains constant. I suspect it will for awhile, but it doesn't matter anymore, because I don't waste my life on things and people I don't have any control over or that don't make any sense. There's plenty of that. However, this time, *"I"* have decided to make sense. That's the difference -- a major difference. I've learned that this is within my power. I may not be able to control external factors and this crazy world, and even crazier human race, but I have the power of response and reaction. I choose to live and survive and see my life the way I want it to be; therefore, it is. I owe it to myself to at least make an effort, every day. This is all that I can do. It's a lot actually. The rest is up to the mysterious universe. I have accepted this and made peace. *Now, on with life!*

I have managed to learn a few things in my 50-plus years of life, which has helped me survive cancer, depression, a neurotic midlife crisis, menopause, ridiculous and cruel people, and other life's insane stuff that never stops happening. And I wanted to share my life lessons that helped me achieve happiness with you, in hopes that you will seek within yourself your own set of life and happy lessons, subtle and yet powerful, derived from your unique life experience and adventures, to help you survive your set of trials and tribulations and keep you moving ahead with dignity, passion, and happiness. It's time to use them. Give yourself credit: You are smart and savvy enough to do it. So, what the heck are you waiting for?

It's funny how something precious can stem from something ugly, painful, dark, tragic and infuriating. But that's just the way it is. It seems in exchange for our suffering, we are offered insights, lessons, and internal beauty in return, to be somewhat fair. It's also an opportunity to make our lives more tolerable, enjoyable, and deeper. It would be a shame to miss all that. It would be the ultimate waste, but so many do.

I realized that I don't have to understand everything or have all the answers. Actually, I understand very little and that's okay. What matters is that my life has meaning, purpose, and happiness. I believe we must experience happiness to say we have truly lived and existed. We were here. It took me more than half a century to discover this, but I am extremely grateful for it.

Some of my greatest life lessons came from my cancer journey. In the midst of unimaginable terror, I've learned that my happiness is innate and I already have it. It's built in. That's the best part. Happiness is within my power, our power. When we choose to be happy with what we have and where we are, it will serve as an incredible tool, to help us survive just about anything in life, as well as help us keep reaching for our hopes and dreams, small or otherwise, and have fun while we're at it. Our happiness also naturally helps others and the world. That alone is worth the effort, but we benefit the most.

We are given a remarkable prize for enduring life's woes and the courage to bear it all. All this can be easily missed in self-pity and denial. So don't do that. We cannot afford it, because we still have a lot of surviving, living, loving, fighting, and giving to do. This is just the beginning.

Open up your mind and continue to learn and challenge yourself. Open your heart to invite love and friendship, build your communities, have compassion for those less fortunate and give them a voice and a hand, and trust your instincts, and take action, and try old and new things to find your own happy methods that will work for you on a daily basis.

I hope I offered you a little something to help you in your own life's journey. Remember, you, life, and happiness will always be evolving, as all things do. So, keep your head up. Don't beat yourself up any more. And if and when you fall, rest, smile, and then get up again and keep moving. You can't fail if you're trying. We have already survived so much, gloriously. Pat yourself on the back. You did it and we'll keep at it. And don't forget to be happy already, now!

Cheers to you, my kindred spirits!
I thank you for your time and wish you a wonderful health and
happiness journey.

Dr. Clara
www.healthhappinessctr.com

Made in the USA
Monee, IL
13 September 2019